INNSBRUCK
Travel Guide
2024/2025

A Complete Pocket Guide to Culture, Top
Attractions, Hidden Treasure and Things to do
in Austria's Alpine Gem

Wendy T. Sierra

Copyright

All rights reserved. No part of this publication may be reproduced, distributed, or transmitted in any form or by any means, including photocopying, recording, or other electronic or mechanical methods, without the prior written permission of the owner.

©[2024][Wendy T. Sierra]

Table of Contents

Copyright..1
Table of Contents..2
Forward... 3
Welcome to Innsbruck..................................... 5
Getting to Innsbruck.......................................13
Where to Stay in Innsbruck............................21
Exploring Innsbruck's Old Town....................30
Must-See Museums & Galleries...................... 41
Outdoor Adventures and Activities................ 51
Day Trips from Innsbruck..............................62
Innsbruck's Culinary Scene........................... 71
Shopping in Innsbruck.................................. 80
Cultural Experiences & Events...................... 90
Family-Friendly Activities..............................99
Nightlife & Entertainment........................... 109
Wellness and Relaxation...............................118
Practical Information for Travelers.............. 128
Sample Itineraries...137
Conclusion.. 148

Forward

The first time I set foot in Innsbruck, I was captivated by the juxtaposition of towering Alpine peaks and a charming city nestled at their base. It was a brisk morning in early winter, and the air was crisp, filled with the scent of fresh snow and the distant echo of church bells. I remember walking through the Old Town, my boots crunching on the cobblestones, as I marveled at the medieval buildings that seemed to whisper stories of emperors and artists, of traders and travelers who had walked these streets long before me.

Innsbruck is a place that invites you to slow down and savor every moment. I recall sitting in a cozy café, sipping a steaming mug of hot chocolate, while outside, the golden roof of the Goldenes Dachl glinted in the sunlight, a beacon of the city's rich history. As I sat there, I couldn't help but feel a deep connection to this place—a city that balances its imperial past with a vibrant, modern culture, all set against the breathtaking backdrop of the Alps.

It was this feeling, this sense of being in a place where history and nature intertwine so effortlessly, that inspired me to create this travel guide. Innsbruck is more than just a destination; it's an experience. Whether you're drawn here by the promise of exhilarating outdoor adventures, the allure of centuries-old architecture, or the warmth of Tyrolean hospitality, there's something in Innsbruck that will resonate with every traveler.

As you explore the pages of this guide, I hope you'll feel a sense of the magic that Innsbruck holds. This is a city that has a way of capturing your heart, of making you feel like you've stumbled upon a hidden gem in the heart of Europe. I invite you to let Innsbruck surprise you, as it has surprised me time and time again. Welcome to Innsbruck—may your journey be as unforgettable as mine.

Welcome to Innsbruck

Nestled in the heart of the Austrian Alps, Innsbruck is a location where nature's magnificence blends effortlessly with a rich cultural past. Whether you're an adventurer looking to climb towering peaks, a history buff looking to wander through centuries-old neighborhoods, or a visitor looking for real European experiences, Innsbruck has something for everyone. This city, recognized for its postcard-perfect vistas, world-class skiing, and thriving cultural scene, is more than simply a stop on your travel schedule; it's a destination that catches your imagination and stays with you long after you leave. As you prepare to tour Innsbruck, you will discover a city that seamlessly mixes the ancient with the new, providing something unique for every sort of traveler.

Introduction to Innsbruck

Innsbruck, the capital of the Tyrol region in western Austria, exudes charm and elegance against the backdrop of the breathtaking Alps. The name "Innsbruck" properly translates to "Bridge over the Inn," referring to the Inn River, which runs beautifully through the city, reflecting both medieval and modern architecture. This city is more than just its natural beauty; it is a vibrant blend of history, culture, and outdoor activities.

Innsbruck is a city of contrasts, where the energy of city life coexists with the serenity of nature. The city's small size makes it easy to explore, yet it is packed with attractions, from the medieval Old Town to cutting-edge architectural wonders. For ages, Innsbruck has been a cultural crossroads, attracting artists, singers, and thinkers from around Europe. Today, it remains a magnet for innovation, education, and tourism, attracting tourists from all over the world seeking to experience its distinct combination of heritage and contemporary.

The city's position in the middle of the Alps makes it a top choice for outdoor enthusiasts. Whether you visit Innsbruck in the winter for world-class skiing or in the summer for hiking and mountain biking, there are a variety of activities available to immerse yourself in the region's natural splendor. Aside from its natural attractions, Innsbruck is a city of culture and history, with museums, galleries, and historical monuments that tell the narrative of its colorful past.

A Brief History of Innsbruck

Innsbruck's history is as intriguing as the city itself, dating back over 800 years. Count Berthold V of Andechs established the city as a market town in 1180, and it became a city in 1239. Its strategic placement on crucial trade routes between Italy and Germany made it a vital commercial and cultural hub.

During the 14th century, Innsbruck became Tyrol's capital, which increased its political and economic prominence dramatically. The Habsburg dynasty, which dominated most of Europe, had a lasting influence on Innsbruck. Emperor Maximilian I is credited with converting Innsbruck into a city of imperial prominence. During his reign, several of the city's prominent monuments were created, notably the Golden Roof (Goldenes Dachl), a symbol commemorating his marriage to Bianca Maria Sforza of Milan.

During the 16th century, the city thrived as an arts and sciences center, drawing intellectuals, painters, and craftspeople. The foundation of the University of Innsbruck in 1669 cemented the city's position as a center of learning and intellectual study.

Innsbruck's history is also defined by its involvement in the Napoleonic Wars and resistance to Bavarian and French control. The Tyrolean Rebellion of 1809, headed by local hero Andreas Hofer, is an important episode in the city's history, representing the people's staunch independence and perseverance.

The twentieth century provided both problems and opportunities to Innsbruck. It hosted the Winter Olympics twice (1964 and 1976), showcasing its world-class alpine facilities and cementing its status as a global winter sports destination. Today, Innsbruck honors its heritage while embracing modernity, providing tourists with a unique perspective on both its past and its vibrant present.

Overview of Local Culture and Traditions

Innsbruck's culture is profoundly anchored in its Alpine environment and Tyrolean background, resulting in a distinct combination of traditions that reflect both the alpine setting and its status as a crossroads of European culture.

Tyrolean Traditions: Innsbruck is the core of Tyrolean culture, famous for its traditional music, dance, and attire. The city routinely holds events and festivals to commemorate this legacy, such as the Tyrolean Evenings, which feature real folk music and dances like the Schuhplattler. Traditional Tyrolean clothes, particularly the dirndl for ladies and lederhosen for men, are commonly worn during these festivities.

Music & Arts: Innsbruck boasts a thriving music culture that spans classical to modern. The city is home to the Innsbruck Festival of Early Music, which draws musicians and listeners from all over the world. Another highlight is the Ambras Castle Concerts, which take place in the beautiful Renaissance castle and feature historical acts. The city's art culture is also vibrant, with various galleries and shows featuring both traditional and modern works.

Cuisine: Tyrolean cuisine is an important aspect of Innsbruck's culture, with substantial meals that are ideal for the chilly mountain environment. Tiroler Gröstl (a fried potato dish with meat), Kaiserschmarrn (shredded pancakes), and Specknödel (bacon dumplings) are all staples. The city's culinary options reflect its status as a cultural melting pot, with restaurants providing a wide range of different cuisines.

Festivals: Throughout the year, Innsbruck hosts events that celebrate its cultural richness. The Christmas markets are very popular, attracting people to the city during the winter months. The markets, set against the background of the snow-covered Alps, sell everything from handmade souvenirs to mulled wine and traditional Tyrolean delicacies. Other prominent events are the Bergisel Ski Jump contests and the New Orleans Festival, which adds jazz to the Alpine city.

Why Visit Innsbruck in 2024/2025?

Innsbruck is always a tempting destination, but 2024 looks to be a particularly exciting year for tourists. Here's why.

New Cultural Attractions: In 2024, numerous new cultural attractions will open in Innsbruck, including the enlarged Tirol Panorama Museum. This museum provides a 360-degree picture of Tyrolean history, along with innovative interactive displays that bring the past to life. New enhancements to the city's art sector are planned, including shows by contemporary artists from around Europe.

Sustainability Initiatives: Innsbruck is at the forefront of sustainable tourism, with new projects aimed at protecting the city's natural environment while improving the guest experience. In 2024, the city will increase its green mobility alternatives, including bike-sharing programs and electric buses, making it simpler than ever to explore Innsbruck without leaving a carbon imprint.

Sporting Events: As a past Winter Olympics host city, Innsbruck is a hub for international athletic events. In 2024, the city will host the European Youth Olympic Festival, which will bring together young athletes from all around the continent. This event, along with the city's year-round outdoor activities, makes Innsbruck a popular destination for sports fans.

Anniversaries and Celebrations: In 2025, Innsbruck will also mark numerous significant anniversaries, including the 201st anniversary of the Bergisel Ski Jump. Special events, concerts, and exhibitions are scheduled throughout the year to honor significant landmarks, allowing visitors to gain a unique perspective on the city's history.

Seasonal Delights: Regardless of when you visit in 2024/2025, Innsbruck has something unique to offer. During the winter, the city changes into a snowy paradise, complete with Christmas markets, ice skating rinks, and adjacent ski resorts. During the summer, the mountains come alive with hiking trails, outdoor concerts, and festivals that highlight the area's natural splendor.

Innsbruck in 2024/2025 combines both adventure and leisure, with a rich history and a forward-thinking outlook, making it ideal for a great holiday. Whether you're a first-time tourist or returning for another visit, Innsbruck is eager to amaze and thrill you with everything it has to offer.

Getting to Innsbruck

Innsbruck's position in the midst of the Alps makes it an attractive destination for those seeking both natural beauty and convenience. Reaching and visiting Innsbruck is a seamless experience, whether you fly in from another country, arrive by rail, drive through breathtaking alpine scenery, or rely on local transit. Here's how to get to and around this picturesque Alpine city.

International Flights to Innsbruck

Innsbruck Airport (INN) is the key international gateway, with direct flights from numerous major European cities and seasonal connections to a variety of worldwide locations. Innsbruck Airport, located just 4 kilometers from the city center, is noted for its dramatic approach, in which planes descend between towering alpine peaks—a thrilling beginning to your stay in the Alps.

Key Connections: Innsbruck is well connected to major centers such as Frankfurt, London, Amsterdam, and Vienna. Austrian Airlines, Lufthansa, British Airways, and easyJet all routinely fly to and from Innsbruck, especially during the peak ski season.

Seasonal Flights: During the winter months, Innsbruck becomes a popular destination for winter sports lovers, with various charter flights catering to skiers and snowboarders from around Europe. In the summer, the airport serves as a gateway for tourists looking for alpine hikes and outdoor experiences, with extra flights from popular destinations.

Transfers from the Airport: Once you've arrived at Innsbruck Airport, getting to the city center is simple. The F bus service runs every 15 minutes and takes you directly from the airport to the main train station (Innsbruck Hauptbahnhof) in approximately 20 minutes. Taxis are widely available, providing a faster, more private ride to your hotel. For those looking for a more environmentally responsible option, several hotels provide shuttle services in electric vehicles.

Arriving by Train: Rail Connections and Services

Arriving in Innsbruck by train is a convenient and picturesque alternative, as the city is a significant stop on numerous major European rail lines. The major rail station, Innsbruck Hauptbahnhof, is ideally positioned in the city center, making it simple to transition from your travel to exploring the city.

European Rail Connections: Innsbruck is well connected to the European rail network, with direct trains from Munich, Zurich, Milan, and Vienna. The travel from Munich, for example, takes around two hours, but Zurich is roughly three and a half hours by rail. Austrian Federal Railways (ÖBB) and Deutsche Bahn (DB) offer frequent services, making it easy for passengers to reach Innsbruck from around Europe.

Scenic Rail Journeys: One of the most enjoyable aspects of taking the train to Innsbruck is the stunning countryside. The roads across the Alps provide breathtaking vistas of snow-capped mountains, verdant valleys, and charming communities. The ride from Zurich, in particular, is known for its breathtaking scenery as the train travels via the Arlberg Pass.

Services & Amenities at Innsbruck Hauptbahnhof: Innsbruck's main rail station is contemporary and well-equipped, including restaurants, shops, and luggage storage areas. From here, you can easily access local transit choices like buses and trams, or you can just walk to your hotel if you are staying in the city center.

Driving to Innsbruck: Routes and Scenic Drives

Driving to Innsbruck allows you to explore the alpine country at your own speed while also enjoying some of Europe's most gorgeous roadways. The city is well-connected by highways, allowing access from many areas of Austria and adjacent countries.

Driving Routes: If you're going from Munich, the A12 and A13 roads will take you to Innsbruck in around two hours. The trip from Zurich takes around three hours, with direct access via the A1 and A12. For travelers driving from Italy, the Brenner Pass is the most important crossing point, with the A22 and E45 roads heading directly into Innsbruck.

Scenic Drives: For those with a little more time, the drive to Innsbruck may be an adventure in itself. If you're traveling from Germany, consider taking the picturesque route through the Fern Pass, or from Switzerland, take the Arlberg Pass. These routes provide breathtaking views of the Alps, with possibilities to visit tiny villages, lakes, and panoramic overlooks along the way.

Parking in Innsbruck: There are numerous parking alternatives available in the city center and on the outskirts. Public parking garages are provided near major sites, and many hotels provide parking for guests. Consider parking at a Park & Ride facility on the city's outskirts, which is accessible to the city center via public transit.

Local Transportation: Buses, Trams and Taxis

Once you arrive in Innsbruck, you can easily navigate the city owing to its fast and well-organized public transit system. Innsbruck's modest size and great public transportation make it easy to explore the city without a car.

Buses and Trams: Innsbruck has a large network of buses and trams managed by the Innsbrucker Verkehrsbetriebe (IVB). The trams are very useful for tourism, as multiple lines run past significant locations of the city. The J line, for example, runs from the city center to the Hungerburg funicular, which links to the Nordkette mountain range. The buses supplement the tram network by providing transportation to places not serviced by trams, such as the neighboring suburbs and towns.

Tickets & Passes: Bus and tram tickets can be purchased from ticket machines at stations or through the IVB app. For guests who want to use public transit regularly, the Innsbruck Card is a fantastic bargain. It offers unrestricted use of public transit throughout the city, as well as free admission to several of Innsbruck's main attractions.

Taxis & Ridesharing: Taxis are easily accessible throughout Innsbruck and may be hailed on the street, ordered over the phone, or via apps. Ridesharing services are also available in Innsbruck, giving yet another handy mode of transportation. Taxis are more expensive than public transit, but they are a faster, more direct mode of transportation, especially if you are carrying luggage or traveling in a group.

Sustainable Travel Options

Innsbruck is a city that prioritizes sustainability, which is evident in its transportation alternatives. Whether you want to reduce your carbon footprint or simply explore the city in a more environmentally responsible way, there are various sustainable travel choices to choose from.

Bike Sharing: Innsbruck is a bike-friendly city with several designated riding pathways and a prominent bike-sharing program known as Stadtrad. The city's small shape makes riding an excellent way to explore, and bikes can be rented at a variety of stations throughout Innsbruck. For those seeking to venture outside the city, various firms rent e-bikes, allowing you to effortlessly navigate the neighboring mountain paths.

Walking: Innsbruck's walkability is one of its numerous attractions. The city core is pedestrian-friendly, with several attractions within easy walking distance of one another. Strolling around the Old Town, with its magnificent buildings and lively squares, is one of the greatest ways to soak up the city's ambiance.

Electric Buses & Trams: Innsbruck's public transportation network includes electric trams and buses, which help to reduce the city's carbon emissions. Electric trams, in particular, are a smooth and quiet mode of transportation that also provides stunning vistas as they drive around the city.

Green Hotels & Eco-Friendly Accommodations: Innsbruck has a variety of eco-friendly lodging options for guests that value sustainability. Many of the city's hotels are devoted to environmental measures, including energy-efficient operations and organic and locally produced cuisine. Staying at one of these green hotels is a terrific way to lessen your environmental footprint while also having a nice stay in Innsbruck.

Getting to Innsbruck and exploring the city is not only convenient, but also an essential element of the whole tourist experience. With a number of alternatives to suit various preferences—whether you're flying in, taking a train, driving, or exploring the city on foot—Innsbruck's accessibility and transportation options set the setting for an unforgettable stay.

Where to Stay in Innsbruck

Innsbruck, set in the Austrian Alps, provides a diverse range of lodgings to suit all sorts of guests. Whether you want the ultimate luxury experience, a low-cost stay, or something special and unforgettable, the city provides something for everyone. Choosing where to stay in Innsbruck depends on the type of experience you seek as well as the comfort and amenities provided. We've broken down the alternatives below to help you choose the best location to stay.

Luxury Hotels and Resorts

For those looking to enjoy the best that Innsbruck has to offer, the city's luxury hotels and resorts provide an unrivaled experience. These hotels blend the elegance of alpine architecture with modern comforts, giving visitors the best of both worlds.

Grand Hotel Europa: This historic hotel, conveniently located near the major train station, combines classic Tyrolean elegance with modern amenities. The rooms are nicely equipped, and the hotel has an on-site restaurant serving gourmet Austrian cuisine. Guests may enjoy facilities such as a wellness center, concierge services, and breathtaking mountain views.

Hotel Schwarzer Adler: Hotel Schwarzer Adler, a landmark in Innsbruck, has been welcoming guests since the 16th century. It's a boutique luxury hotel with a long history, and each room is distinctively designed to blend classic elegance with modern amenities. The rooftop patio has beautiful views of the Alps, and the spa offers a peaceful respite after a day of touring the city.

NALA Individuellhotel: NALA Individuellhotel is a premium boutique hotel known for its artistic flair, inventive design, and customized service. Each room is distinctively furnished, providing visitors with a unique experience. The hotel's dedication to sustainability is evident in its organic breakfast options and environmentally friendly services.

Staying at one of these luxury hotels not only gives high-end comfort but also places you in great locations, whether in the center of the city or with panoramic views of the surrounding mountains.

Budget-Friendly Accommodations

Innsbruck offers a variety of budget-friendly accommodations that do not sacrifice luxury or convenience. These lodgings are great for individuals who want to make the most of their vacation without splurging on housing.

Hotel Zillertal: Situated just outside the city center, Hotel Zillertal provides cheap accommodations with convenient access to public transit. The rooms are clean, comfy, and provide basic facilities. The hotel also offers a free breakfast, making it an excellent choice for budget-conscious guests.

Motel One Innsbruck: This trendy budget hotel brand provides elegant yet economical lodgings in the city core. Motel One Innsbruck is noted for its modern architecture, cozy rooms, and lively lobby area where guests may unwind or work. The hotel's central position makes it convenient to explore the city on foot.

Youth Hostel Innsbruck: For backpackers and young visitors, Youth Hostel Innsbruck provides dormitory-style lodgings for a fraction of the price of a hotel. The hostel is near the Olympic Village and has convenient access to both the city core and outdoor activities. It's a terrific way to meet other travelers and share your experiences.

These affordable solutions ensure that you can enjoy everything Innsbruck has to offer while keeping your lodging costs low.

Boutique Hotels and Unique Stays

For guests seeking something more special, Innsbruck's boutique hotels and unique rooms provide a one-of-a-kind experience. These locations frequently mix personalized service with a unique flair that distinguishes them from typical hotels.

Weisses Rössl: Located in the center of Innsbruck's Old Town, Weisses Rössl is a delightful boutique hotel in a historic structure. The rooms combine classic Tyrolean décor with modern facilities, and the hotel's restaurant is well-known for its genuine Austrian cuisine. Staying here feels like going back in time while enjoying all of the modern conveniences.

Stage 12 Hotel by Penz: This trendy boutique hotel has contemporary decor in a prime location just a stone's throw from the Golden Roof. Stage 12 mixes modern elegance with a relaxed ambiance, making it an ideal choice for tourists looking to be in the heart of Innsbruck's dynamic city scene. The hotel's bar is a favorite hangout for both residents and guests, providing a stylish atmosphere to unwind.

Adlers Hotel: For those wanting a contemporary, urban experience with a twist, Adlers Hotel provides a room with a view. This boutique hotel is the highest in Innsbruck, with rooms offering panoramic views of the city and surrounding mountains. The hotel's rooftop bar and restaurant are famous for both the food and the breathtaking views.

These boutique hotels and unusual accommodations are ideal for tourists looking for an out-of-the-ordinary experience in Innsbruck, with unforgettable details that make your stay exceptional.

Family-Friendly Accommodations

Traveling with family necessitates lodgings that provide comfort, space, and facilities suitable for all ages. Innsbruck features a number of family-friendly hotels and apartments that will make everyone's stay enjoyable, from infants to grandparents.

Austria Trend Hotel Congress Innsbruck: Located near the Congress and Messe Innsbruck, this hotel is ideal for families. The rooms and suites are large, with lots of space for children to play, and the hotel provides facilities such as a playground, babysitter services, and family-friendly restaurants.

Alpenpark Resort Seefeld: Located somewhat outside of Innsbruck in adjacent Seefeld, Alpenpark Resort is a good option for families. It provides a variety of activities for children, such as a kids' club, swimming pools, and outdoor playgrounds. The resort's family accommodations are well-equipped, and the surrounding region offers many outdoor activities.

Apartment Hotels: For families that want a more home-like atmosphere, numerous apartment hotels in Innsbruck provide self-catering accommodations with full kitchens and separate bedrooms. These are great for extended stays or families that want to make their own meals. Rufi's Hotel & Apartments is an example of an apartment hotel that offers the convenience of hotel amenities while maintaining the comfort of an apartment.

These family-friendly alternatives ensure that both parents and children can unwind and enjoy their time in Innsbruck, with all of the comforts and conveniences required for a stress-free getaway.

Staying in the Old Town vs. Outskirts: Pros and Cons

When deciding where to stay in Innsbruck, one of the most important considerations is whether to stay in the historic Old Town or on the city's outskirts. Each option provides a unique experience, and your pick will be based on your interests and travel objectives.

Staying in the Old Town: The center of Innsbruck is the Old Town (Altstadt), which has cobblestone streets, ancient buildings, and renowned monuments such as the Golden Roof and the Hofburg. Staying here puts you within walking distance of the city's main attractions, restaurants, and shopping. The atmosphere is energetic and colorful, especially in the evenings when the streets are bustling with both residents and visitors. However, hotels in the Old Town might be more expensive, and the neighborhood can be crowded, particularly during high tourist seasons.

- **Pros:**
    - Proximity to key attractions.
    - Charming, historic atmosphere.
    - Easy access to eating and shopping.
- **Cons:**
    - Higher lodging expenses.
    - Potential for noise, especially at night.
    - Limited parking choices.

Staying in the Outskirts: Innsbruck's outskirts provide a calmer, more relaxed environment, as well as breathtaking mountain vistas. Accommodations here are frequently more spacious and inexpensive, yet you can still easily access the city center via public transit. The outskirts are great for those looking to combine city discovery with outdoor activities like hiking, skiing, or simply admiring the region's natural splendor.

- **Pros:**
    - Quieter, more relaxed atmosphere
    - Reduced lodging expenses.
    - Easy access to outdoor activities.
- **Cons:**
    - Further from the city attractions.

- Dependence on public transportation or a car
- There are fewer restaurants and entertainment alternatives nearby.

What you want out of your time in Innsbruck will determine whether you choose the Old Town or the suburbs. Whether you like the busy, historic charm of the city center or the quiet serenity of the surrounding mountains, Innsbruck has something for every visitor.

No matter where you stay in Innsbruck, the city's many lodging options ensure that you'll find a hotel that meets your needs, budget, and travel style. Whether you're looking for luxury, a budget-friendly choice, or a one-of-a-kind experience, Innsbruck's numerous hotel options will give the ideal starting point for your alpine journey.

Exploring Innsbruck's Old Town

Innsbruck's Old Town, or Altstadt, is the city's historic center and a treasure trove of cultural, architectural, and historical attractions. As you walk through its small alleyways, you'll be taken back in time, surrounded by structures that have stood for centuries and each tell a unique tale. The Old Town brings Innsbruck's rich history to life, with surprising discoveries around every turn. Exploring the Old Town is a leisurely experience, with prominent structures like the Golden Roof and hidden courtyards whispering tales of bygone periods. Let's look at some of the must-see sites and lesser-known gems that make Innsbruck's Old Town so unique.

The Golden Roof (Goldenes Dachl)

The Golden Roof is undoubtedly the most recognizable emblem of Innsbruck and a must-see for anybody visiting the city. Located in the center of the Old Town, this majestic monument is a tribute to the city's imperial heritage and is frequently the first stop for travelers.

Emperor Maximilian I commissioned the Golden Roof in the early 16th century to commemorate his marriage to Bianca Maria Sforza. The roof is coated in 2,657 fire-gilded copper tiles, giving it a characteristic golden sheen. The edifice functioned as a royal box from which the emperor and his entourage could watch festivals, tournaments, and other public events taking place in the plaza below.

Today, the Golden Roof holds a modest museum devoted to Emperor Maximilian I, where visitors may learn about his life and the building's history. As you stand in front of this majestic monument, you can easily visualize the majesty of imperial Innsbruck and the significance of this location in the city's history.

Innsbruck Cathedral (Dom zu St. Jakob)

The beautiful Innsbruck Cathedral, also known as the Cathedral of St. James, is only a short walk away from the Golden Roof. This baroque

masterpiece is one of Tyrol's most prominent ecclesiastical buildings and a must-see in the Old Town.

The cathedral was initially erected in the 12th century, but it underwent substantial renovations in the early 18th century, giving it its modern baroque aspect. The cathedral's interior is stunning, with beautiful murals, golden altars, and delicate stucco work that represent the craftsmanship of the time. One of the cathedral's most famous elements is the high altar, which includes a painting by Lucas Cranach the Elder of the Madonna and Child. This picture is said to be magical, drawing pilgrims from all around the region.

Visitors can also pay their respects at the grave of Archduke Maximilian III, who was the Grand Master of the Teutonic Order and is buried in the cathedral's crypt. The cathedral's two bell towers, which dominate the Innsbruck skyline, are another notable feature. A visit to Innsbruck Cathedral provides a tranquil respite from the activity of the Old Town, enabling you to contemplate on the city's spiritual legacy.

The Hofburg Imperial Palace

A short walk from the cathedral leads to the Hofburg Imperial Palace, one of Innsbruck's most prominent cultural and historical monuments. For centuries, the Hofburg, the Habsburgs' former palace, has been central to

Tyrolean history. Built in the 15th century, the

palace has been enlarged and rebuilt over the years, most notably by Empress Maria Theresa, who gave it its present baroque and rococo form.

The palace is divided into numerous sections, including the state apartments, the Empress Elisabeth Apartment, and the Giant Hall (Riesensaal), all of which provide insight into the Habsburgs' lavish lifestyle. The Giant Hall, with its beautiful ceiling paintings and crystal chandeliers, is particularly remarkable and has hosted significant official occasions and banquets.

As you tour the Hofburg, you'll come across displays that explain the history of the Habsburg dynasty and their effect on the region. The royal grounds, with their well groomed grass and baroque statuary, offer a peaceful location to unwind and reflect on your stay.

Visiting the Hofburg Imperial Palace is like stepping into a time machine, providing an intriguing glimpse into the grandeur of the Habsburg era and Innsbruck's role as a regional center of power.

Maria-Theresien-Straße: Innsbruck's Most Famous Street

No visit to Innsbruck's Old Town is complete without a trip along Maria-Theresien-Straße, the city's most well-known and colorful street. Named for Empress Maria Theresa, this large avenue is dotted with ancient buildings, shops, cafés, and restaurants, making it the ideal area to take in the city's ambiance.

Maria-Theresien-Straße has been the major street in Innsbruck since the 18th century, and it remains the center of the city's social life. The street is lined with stunning baroque and rococo structures, many of which have been scrupulously kept, lending the neighborhood a timeless beauty.

As you go along the street, you'll cross the Annasäule, a column built in 1706 to mark Tyrol's emancipation from Bavarian rule. The column is topped by a figure of the Virgin Mary, who is considered as the region's protector. The Triumphal Arch, located at the southern end of Maria-Theresien-Straße, was commissioned by Maria Theresa to honor her son Leopold II's marriage.

Maria-Theresien-Straße is also a shopping hotspot, featuring a mix of high-end boutiques, local artisan businesses, and worldwide brands. This lively street provides something for everyone, whether you're seeking a unique item or simply want to relax with a coffee while people-watching.

Innsbruck City Tower (Stadtturm)

The Innsbruck City Tower (Stadtturm) offers panoramic views of Innsbruck's Old Town and the surrounding Alps. This ancient tower, dating back to the 15th century, was formerly part of the city's fortifications and functioned as an observation point for watchmen monitoring the city's activity.

The tower is 51 meters tall, and after climbing the 148 steps to the observation deck, you will be rewarded with stunning views of the city and the mountains beyond. The ascent itself is an experience, as the narrow, twisting staircase leads you past centuries-old walls and small windows that provide views of the city as you rise.

The views from the summit include the red-roofed houses of the Old Town, the spires of the Innsbruck Cathedral, and the Hofburg Imperial Palace. The vista also includes the Nordkette mountain range, which gives a beautiful background to the city.

The Innsbruck City Tower is not only an excellent spot to enjoy the city's splendor, but it also provides insight into Innsbruck's history and role as a regional strategic and cultural hub.

Hidden Gems in the Old Town: Small Alleys and Courtyards

While the famous sights of Innsbruck's Old Town are well worth seeing, some of the most unforgettable experiences may be had by just venturing off the usual route. The Old Town is crisscrossed with small passageways and secret courtyards that tourists sometimes ignore but provide insight into the city's lesser-known past.

Kiebachgasse: This tiny alley near the Golden Roof is dotted with colorful buildings and little stores that have existed for decades. Walking down Kiebachgasse seems like stepping back in time, since the buildings' historic façade and wooden shutters remain intact. The lane leads to the Ottoburg, one of Innsbruck's oldest buildings, which presently serves as a traditional Tyrolean restaurant.

Stadtsäle Innsbruck Courtyard: Tucked away behind the Hofburg, this peaceful courtyard is a hidden gem in the heart of the Old Town. The courtyard is surrounded by ancient buildings and includes a small fountain as well as seating spots for visitors to take a break from exploring. It's a quiet place to experience the splendor of Innsbruck without the throng.

Pfarrgasse: Another delightful lane in the Old Town, Pfarrgasse is famous for its modest cafés and stores. The alley is most picturesque in the early morning or late afternoon, when the sun forms long shadows on the cobblestone streets. It's the ideal spot to discover local crafts or sip a coffee while taking in the atmosphere of the Old Town.

Exploring these hidden jewels provides a more intimate view of Innsbruck, allowing you to interact with the city's history in a unique and important way. As you explore these lesser-known areas, you'll discover that Innsbruck's Old Town is full of surprises, with each turn exposing a new piece of the city's rich cultural fabric.

Innsbruck's Old Town combines history, culture, and architecture to offer a genuinely unique experience. Whether you're gazing at the Golden Roof, visiting the vast halls of the Hofburg, or simply getting lost in the maze of streets and courtyards, the Old Town has something for everyone. It's a spot where history and the present mix, making it a must-see for anybody visiting Innsbruck.

Must-See Museums & Galleries

Innsbruck, with its rich cultural past and dynamic artistic scene, is a sanctuary for museums and art lovers alike. The city's museums and galleries offer a thorough dive into Tyrolean history, art, and science, making them must-see sites for anybody wishing to enrich their vacation. From experiencing the history of the Habsburg Empire to finding contemporary art, Innsbruck's cultural institutions offer something to pique your curiosity. Here's a list of some of the most interesting museums and galleries you should visit.

Tiroler Landesmuseum Ferdinandeum

The Tiroler Landesmuseum Ferdinandeum, often known as the Ferdinandeum, is one of Innsbruck's most prestigious cultural institutions and a treasure mine of Tyrolean art and history. Established in 1823, it is one of Austria's oldest museums, providing a thorough picture of the region's artistic and cultural history from prehistoric to present times.

The museum's collection is extensive and diversified, comprising various departments:

Prehistoric & Early History: Discover Bronze Age, Roman, and early medieval artifacts that give information on the region's old civilizations.

Art History: The Ferdinandeum houses an extraordinary collection of medieval and baroque art, including works by Tyrolean masters like Michael Pacher and Paul Troger. The collection also includes several Gothic altarpieces and Renaissance artworks.

Modern & Contemporary Art: For visitors interested in more recent artistic styles, the museum's modern art collection includes works by notable 19th and 20th-century painters such as Egon Schiele and Oskar Kokoschka. Temporary shows frequently include modern Austrian artists, giving the Ferdinandeum a lively place to see the progress of art.

Music and Folk Art: The museum also holds a large collection of musical instruments and folk art, which provide insight into Tyrolean traditional crafts and customs.

Visiting the Ferdinandeum gives a comprehensive grasp of Tyrol's cultural legacy, making it a must-see for history aficionados and art enthusiasts alike.

The Imperial Palace Museum

The Imperial Palace Museum, housed within the Hofburg Imperial Palace, provides an intriguing look into the Habsburgs' lavish lifestyle and the history of the Austrian monarchy. As you tour the museum, you'll be transported back in time to an age of grandeur and imperial authority, with each chamber showing a distinct facet of royal life. The key attractions of the museum include:

The State Apartments: These ornately adorned apartments were once utilized for formal occasions and ceremonies. The Giant Hall (Riesensaal), with its sparkling chandeliers and enormous ceiling paintings, is especially spectacular and has served as the focal point for state dinners and festivities.

The Empress Elisabeth Apartment: This area of the museum is dedicated to Empress Elisabeth, popularly known as Sisi, and offers a glimpse into the private life of one of Austria's most revered and mysterious royalty. Personal possessions, pictures, and letters provide a profound glimpse into Sisi's life and legacy.

The Ancestral Gallery: This gallery contains pictures of the Habsburg dynasty, which trace the ancestry of one of Europe's most influential dynasties. The pictures are complemented by extensive accounts of each ruler's accomplishments and services to the empire.

The museum frequently offers temporary exhibitions that explore various areas of Habsburg history, so there is always something new to learn. A visit to the Imperial Palace Museum not only broadens your awareness of Innsbruck's history, but also transports you to the majesty of the Habsburg era.

The Grassmayr Bell Museum

The Grassmayr Bell Museum provides a genuinely unique cultural experience by

allowing visitors to study the art and science of bell-making. The museum is part of the Grassmayr Bell Foundry, a family-owned enterprise that has been casting bells for almost 400 years, making it one of the world's oldest.

The museum takes visitors through the whole bell-making process, from design and molding to casting and tuning. Highlights include:

Historical Bell Collection: Discover a collection of bells from many ages and countries, each with a unique tale. The collection explores the history of bell-making processes as well as the cultural importance of bells in many societies.

Interactive Exhibits: The museum has various hands-on displays where visitors may explore with sound and acoustics, discovering how a bell's shape and size affect its tone. This participatory approach makes the museum appealing to visitors of all ages.

The Foundry Workshop: See the traditional workmanship that goes into making each bell. The workshop section allows visitors to observe artists at work, giving an intriguing glimpse into a craft that has remained mostly untouched for decades.

The Grassmayr Bell Museum is more than simply a museum; it is a living example of a centuries-old heritage that is still thriving in Innsbruck. Whether you're interested in history, art, or science, this museum provides an unforgettable experience.

The Audioversum ScienceCenter

Unlike many of Innsbruck's museums, which are historically focused, the Audioversum ScienceCenter is a cutting-edge interactive museum dedicated to the realm of sound and hearing. Located in the center of Innsbruck, the Audioversum is an immersive experience that combines science, art, and technology to investigate the secrets of sound. The Audioversum has several key characteristics, including:

Interactive Exhibits: The museum is full of hands-on displays that allow visitors to experiment with sound in new ways. The Audioversum provides an entertaining and instructive experience for people of all ages, from making their own soundscapes to learning about the mechanics of sound waves.

The Sound Lab: This area of the museum focuses on the science of hearing, providing insights into how the human ear works and how we perceive sound. Visitors may use interactive displays to test their hearing, experience what it's like to suffer hearing loss, and learn about the newest breakthroughs in hearing equipment.

Art and Sound Installations: The Audioversum also has various art pieces that investigate the interaction between sound and visual arts. These installations encourage visitors to think about sound in new and innovative ways, transforming the museum into a hub for both scientific discovery and artistic inspiration.

The Audioversum ScienceCenter is a must-see for anybody interested in sound science or seeking a fun museum experience for the whole family. Its unique exhibits make learning about sound enjoyable and accessible, ensuring that visitors of all ages leave with a better understanding of how sound affects our lives.

Art Galleries: Showcasing Local and Contemporary Art

Innsbruck has a thriving art culture, with various galleries showing both local and modern art. These galleries provide an insight into the city's creative pulse, showcasing the work of both Tyrolean and worldwide artists.

Galerie im Taxispalais: Housed in a historic palace in the Old Town, Galerie im Taxispalais is one of Innsbruck's premier modern art galleries. The gallery features alternating exhibitions of modern art in a variety of disciplines, including painting, sculpture, video, and installation art. It's a dynamic place that encourages conversation between artists and the general public, serving as a regional focus for modern art.

Kunstpavillon: Located in Rapoldi Park, the Kunstpavillon is another significant venue for contemporary art in Innsbruck. The gallery specializes in experimental and avant-garde art, offering a venue for budding artists to display their work. The shows here frequently challenge the boundaries of traditional art, making it a must-see for anyone seeking cutting-edge artistic expression.

Galerie Bernd Kugler: For individuals interested in modern photography and fine art, Galerie Bernd Kugler is an excellent choice. The gallery represents a diverse group of recognized and young artists, with a particular emphasis on photography and conceptual art. The shows are meticulously designed to provide visitors with a thought-provoking and visually appealing experience.

These galleries, along with many others in Innsbruck, demonstrate the city's dedication to cultivating a vibrant arts culture. Whether you're an experienced art collector or just like the beauty of visual art, Innsbruck's galleries provide a diverse and interesting experience.

Innsbruck's museums and galleries are more than simply places to see art and history; they are immersive settings that allow you to interact with the city's diverse cultural scene. From the stately halls of the Hofburg to the interactive exhibitions of the Audioversum, each institution provides a distinct view of Innsbruck's past, present, and future. Whether you're a history buff, an art lover, or simply interested, seeing Innsbruck's cultural attractions will definitely enrich your visit to this stunning Alpine city.

Outdoor Adventures and Activities

Innsbruck is a sanctuary for outdoor enthusiasts, with a diverse choice of activities suitable for all seasons. The city, located in the heart of the Austrian Alps, offers easy access to spectacular natural surroundings, making it a perfect destination for both thrill-seekers and those wishing to reconnect with nature. Whether you travel in the summer or winter, Innsbruck's outdoor experiences will provide a unique experience. In this chapter, we'll look at some of the most fascinating things you should include on your agenda.

Hiking in the Nordkette Mountains

The Nordkette mountain range, part of the greater Karwendel Alps, provides a spectacular backdrop for Innsbruck and some of the greatest hiking options in the area. The Nordkette is a hiker's paradise, with paths ranging from easy treks to demanding climbs.

Easy to Moderate Hikes: For those looking for a relaxing stroll with beautiful vistas, the Zirbenweg Trail is a popular alternative. This track, accessible by the Patscherkofel or Glungezer lifts, winds through old pine trees and provides panoramic views of the Inn Valley below. The trail is generally level, making it ideal for families and inexperienced hikers.

Advanced Hikes: More experienced hikers can take on the Goetheweg Trail, which begins at Hafelekar station. This path provides a more difficult ascent with breathtaking views of the rough alpine scenery. The trail brings you near to the Nordkette's high peaks, and reaching the summit gives you a sense of accomplishment.

Alpine Flora and Fauna: Hikers can enjoy the various mountain flora and potentially see animals such as marmots and chamois. The Nordkette also has various mountain cabins where you can relax and eat traditional Tyrolean cuisine while taking in the scenery.

Hiking in the Nordkette is about more than simply physical exertion; it's about immersing yourself in the Alps' calm splendor. Whether you're an experienced hiker or a casual stroll, the Nordkette provides something for everyone.

Skiing and Snowboarding: Innsbruck's Best Slopes

Innsbruck is widely regarded as one of Europe's best winter sports destinations, and with good reason. The city is bordered by many world-class ski resorts that cater to skiers and snowboarders of all abilities. Whether you're a beginner or an expert, the slopes in Innsbruck provide limitless chances for winter pleasure.

Nordkette Ski Resort: For those who want to combine skiing with breathtaking city views, the Nordkette Ski Resort is an excellent choice. This resort, located just a short cable car ride from the city center, provides steep slopes that are especially popular with expert skiers. The Hafelekar run, with its steep ascent, is a must-do for adrenaline enthusiasts.

Patscherkofel Ski Resort: Located just south of Innsbruck, Patscherkofel Ski Resort is suitable for families and novices. The resort's large, mellow slopes are ideal for beginning to ski or snowboard. Patscherkofel has a lengthy history of winter sports, having held events in the 1964 and 1976 Winter Olympics.

Axamer Lizum: Often known as the "White Roof of Innsbruck," Axamer Lizum is another popular winter sports destination. Axamer Lizum is a popular destination for both residents and visitors, with slopes ranging from beginner to expert and off-piste options for the more adventurous. The resort also provides breathtaking views of the neighboring hills and valleys.

In addition to skiing and snowboarding, many Innsbruck resorts include additional winter activities including snowshoeing, tobogganing, and ice skating. The winter season in Innsbruck is particularly spectacular, with a joyful spirit that spreads from the slopes to the city's Christmas markets.

Paragliding & Adventure Sports

For those looking for an adrenaline rush, Innsbruck has a variety of adventure sports that take use of the city's alpine backdrop. Paragliding, in particular, offers a unique perspective on the gorgeous landscapes of Tyrol.

Paragliding: One of the most popular paragliding locations is the Nordkette, where you may take off from the Hafelekar hill and fly down over the city. Tandem paragliding is accessible for individuals with little expertise, allowing you to experience the thrill of flight while admiring the panoramic vistas of the mountains and valleys below. The sensation of soaring into the air with the Alps as your backdrop is one you'll never forget.

Climbing & Via Ferrata: The mountains surrounding Innsbruck provide good prospects for climbing and via ferrata (protected climbing routes). The Nordkette and surrounding Stubai Valley provide a variety of courses for riders of all ability levels. These routes are fitted with fixed cables and ladders, making them suitable for both beginners and experienced climbers.

White Water Rafting: During the warmer months, the rivers near Innsbruck offer spectacular whitewater rafting adventures. The Inn River and its tributaries provide a variety of rapids, ranging from mild currents appropriate for families to demanding whitewater for adrenaline enthusiasts.

Innsbruck's adventure sports culture is ideal for individuals wishing to test their boundaries and see the Alps from a new viewpoint. Whether you're flying through the skies or navigating a rushing river, these activities provide an unparalleled opportunity to see the region's natural splendor.

The Innsbruck Alpine Zoo

The Innsbruck Alpine Zoo, located on the slopes of the Nordkette mountain range, is one of Europe's highest zoos, providing a one-of-a-kind opportunity to witness alpine animals in a breathtaking natural setting. The zoo is home to a variety of Alps-native species, providing an instructive and fun experience for visitors of all ages.

Alpine Fauna: The zoo's occupants comprise more than 150 species, including ibex, lynx, brown bears, and golden eagles. Each enclosure is meant to simulate the animals' native habitat, allowing visitors to experience them in surroundings similar to the wild. The zoo also has a large collection of alpine fish, amphibians, and reptiles.

Educational Exhibits: The Innsbruck Alpine

Zoo emphasizes education and conservation. Interactive exhibits and instructional displays help visitors understand the problems that alpine species face, as well as the need of protecting their ecosystems. The zoo also provides guided tours and educational activities for children and adults.

Stunning Views: In addition to wildlife, the zoo provides breathtaking views of Innsbruck and the surrounding Alps. The zoo's placement on a hillside allows visitors to enjoy spectacular views while viewing the many exhibits.

The Innsbruck mountain Zoo is a must-see for families and environment enthusiasts, with a unique combination of species and breathtaking mountain landscape. It's an ideal way to spend the day taking in the region's natural beauties.

Cycling & Mountain Biking Routes

Innsbruck's diversified geography makes it an ideal location for cycling aficionados, whether they like leisurely rides down the valley or difficult mountain bike tracks. The city and its surroundings provide a diverse choice of paths ideal for all abilities.

Inntal Cycle Path: For those who love picturesque, leisurely rides, the Inntal Cycle Path is an excellent choice. This route runs along the Inn River, passing through scenic villages, lush fields, and historical landmarks. It's a moderately flat trail, making it suitable for cyclists of all ages and abilities. You may rent bikes in Innsbruck and spend the day exploring the breathtaking Tyrolean landscape at your leisure.

Mountain Biking Trails: For more daring bikers, the mountains around Innsbruck provide a plethora of exciting mountain riding paths. The Nordkette Singletrail, one of Europe's longest and most difficult routes, is a favorite among advanced riders. The track begins at the Seegrube station and drops over 1000 meters over steep terrain, providing an exciting ride with breathtaking vistas.

E-Bike Tours: If you want to experience the mountains without working up a sweat, e-bike trips are an excellent choice. Innsbruck offers multiple e-bike rental businesses, and guided excursions are offered for people who wish to explore the region with a professional. E-bikes make it simpler to climb inclines, allowing you to appreciate the view without becoming exhausted.

Cycling and mountain riding in Innsbruck provide an excellent balance of fitness and adventure, allowing you to see the region's natural beauty from a new viewpoint.

Summer and Winter: Seasonal Activities in Innsbruck

One of the best things about Innsbruck is that it is a year-round destination, with a diverse choice of activities accessible both in the summer and winter. This bustling Alpine city has enough to offer visitors at any time.

Summer Activities: Summer activities include hiking, cycling, and water sports. The rich green landscapes of the Tyrol area come to life, offering limitless options for outdoor adventure. The crystal-clear lakes near Innsbruck, such as Lake Natterer and Lake Lans, are ideal for swimming, boating, and picnics. Summer provides a variety of festivals and activities, such as outdoor concerts, farmers' markets, and traditional Tyrolean festivities.

Winter Activities: When winter approaches, Innsbruck becomes a winter paradise. In addition to skiing and snowboarding, tourists can enjoy ice skating, snowshoeing, and horse-drawn sleigh rides. The city's Christmas markets are a seasonal highlight, creating a wonderful scene with dazzling lights, festive decorations, and the smells of mulled wine and gingerbread. Winter sports fans will discover a variety of après-ski alternatives, ranging from quaint mountain lodges to bustling bars in the city center.

Innsbruck's capacity to provide such a varied selection of activities year-round distinguishes it as a really unique location. Whether you prefer the snowy slopes or the sunny hiking paths, there is always plenty to do in this picturesque Alpine city.

Outdoor experiences and activities in Innsbruck are integral to the city's unique character. There are several opportunities to interact with nature and appreciate the breathtaking landscapes that surround Innsbruck, ranging from the adrenaline-pumping excitement of paragliding to the quiet serenity of a mountain climb. Whether you travel in the summer or the winter, these activities will leave you with lasting memories of your time in the heart of the Alps.

Day Trips from Innsbruck

Innsbruck is not just a location with its own charms, but it also serves as an excellent starting point for exploring the neighboring Tyrolean area. Within a short drive or train trip, you may see a wide range of landscapes, from medieval towns and cultural treasures to pure natural areas and world-class ski resorts. This chapter will walk you through five of the greatest day excursions from Innsbruck, each giving a distinct perspective on the beauty and history of Austria and beyond.

The Swarovski Crystal Worlds in Wattens

A visit to the Swarovski Crystal Worlds (Swarovski Kristallwelten) in Wattens is like entering a magnificent world of shimmering imagination. This legendary destination, just 20 kilometers from Innsbruck, blends art, innovation, and the sparkling appeal of Swarovski crystals to create a memorable experience.

The Giant's Head & Entrance: Visitors are greeted by the beautiful entryway, which is carved into a grassy hillside and has crystal eyes that gleam in the sunlight. Water flows from the giant's mouth into a mirrored pool, setting the tone for the mysterious adventure that awaits within.

The Chambers of Wonder: Inside, you'll find the Chambers of Wonder, a collection of art installations made by some of the world's most well-known artists and designers. Each chamber presents a distinct version of crystal art, ranging from immersive light shows to detailed sculptures. Highlights include the Crystal Dome, which features 595 mirrors that create a kaleidoscope image, and the Ice Passage, which uses crystal and light to convey the beauty and fragility of ice.

The Garden of the Giant: After visiting the rooms, spend some time wandering about the Garden of the Giant. This outdoor area is full of interactive works, including the Crystal Cloud, a magnificent display of 800,000 hand-mounted crystals that shimmer in the air. The garden also has a playground, maze, and café, making it an excellent destination for families.

A day trip to Swarovski Crystal Worlds transports you into a world where art and crystal collide, providing a captivating experience for people of all ages. This attraction is a must-see for anybody who enjoys art, is a Swarovski enthusiast, or is simply searching for something unusual.

Seefeld in Tirol: A Perfect Alpine Getaway

Seefeld, a lovely mountain hamlet in Tirol, is only a 30-minute drive or train ride from Innsbruck and provides the ideal retreat from the metropolis. Seefeld, known for its breathtaking natural beauty and outdoor activities, is a year-round vacation with something for everyone.

Summer Activities: During the summer months, Seefeld is a popular destination for hikers, bikers, and nature enthusiasts. The community is surrounded by a network of well-marked paths that cater to all skill levels, from easy walks around the Wildsee Lake to strenuous treks in the Karwendel and Wetterstein Mountains. For those seeking a more leisurely vacation, the hamlet has gorgeous gardens, a golf course, and a range of health alternatives such as spas and thermal baths.

Winter Wonderland: In the winter, Seefeld changes into a snowy wonderland renowned for its superb cross-country skiing facilities. The region has approximately 245 kilometers of perfectly groomed tracks, making it one of Europe's top cross-country skiing destinations. Seefeld also provides downhill skiing, snowshoeing, and even ice skating on the frozen Wildsee Lake. The village's stunning Christmas markets and comfortable mountain cottages enhance the festive ambiance.

Cultural Attractions: Beyond its recreational activities, Seefeld has a rich cultural past. Visit the Parish Church of St. Oswald, a stunning specimen of Tyrolean Baroque architecture, or stroll around the village's pedestrian zone to discover local shops and cafés. Seefeld's combination of natural beauty, outdoor activity, and cultural charm makes it an excellent day trip destination for anyone seeking to experience the typical alpine lifestyle.

Hall in Tirol: A Medieval Town

Hall in Tirol, located just 10 kilometers east of Innsbruck, is a wonderfully preserved medieval village that transports visitors back in time. Hall, with its cobblestone lanes, antique buildings, and rich history, is a veritable architectural and cultural treasure trove.

The Mint Tower (Münzerturm): Hall is arguably most known for its history as a minting town, producing the first big silver currency, the thaler. Visit the Mint Tower to learn about the history of coin creation and even create your own souvenir coin. The tower also provides panoramic views of the town and the surrounding mountains, making it an ideal location for photography.

St. Nicholas Church: St. Nicholas Church is another highlight, with its spectacular Gothic architecture. The church's interior boasts stunning paintings, a lavishly designed altar, and elaborate stained-glass windows. It's a calm location to ponder and admire historical workmanship.

Burg Hasegg and the Museum Münze Hall: Visit Burg Hasegg, a medieval castle that currently serves as the Museum Münze Hall. The museum has intriguing displays on the history of coin minting and the town's development. The castle's courtyards and halls are especially worth examining, since they provide insight into medieval life.

Medieval Streets and Markets: Hall's old town is a maze of small lanes, charming squares, and exquisitely maintained structures.

Wander the streets, stop by the weekly farmers' market, and have a coffee at one of the numerous classic cafés. The town's dynamic atmosphere, along with its rich history, make Hall in Tirol a must-see for both history fans and cultural enthusiasts.

The Stubai Glacier: A Year-Round Ski Destination

For visitors looking for a day of skiing or snowboarding, the Stubai Glacier provides some of the greatest conditions in Austria. The glacier, which is only a 45-minute drive from Innsbruck, is open all year and has slopes for skiers of all ability levels.

Skiing & Snowboarding: The Stubai Glacier is Austria's largest glacier ski resort, with more than 110 kilometers of slopes. Whether you're a novice searching for easy runs or an experienced looking for tough descents, the Stubai Glacier has something for you. The resort is recognized for its consistent snow conditions, with skiing available from October to June. The Top of Tyrol viewing platform, at 3,210 meters, provides stunning panoramic views of the surrounding peaks and valleys.

Other Winter Sports: Aside from skiing, the Stubai Glacier provides a range of other winter sports. Try your hand at snowshoeing, tobogganing, or ice climbing, all of which may be scheduled through local guides. The resort also has a snow park for freestylers and a children's section for families.

Summer Glacier Activities: Even during the summer, the Stubai Glacier provides a variety of activities. Hike through the glacial scenery, go on a guided ice cave trip, or simply enjoy the breathtaking views from the numerous hiking routes that crisscross the region. The glacier is also a popular place for paragliding, which provides an exciting opportunity to see the alpine beauty.

The Stubai Glacier is an ideal day excursion for anybody wishing to experience the excitement of the Alps, whether via winter sports or summer experiences.

Visiting the Brenner Pass and the Italian Border

Traveling to the Brenner Pass provides not only breathtaking alpine scenery, but also the unique experience of crossing one of Europe's most recognized frontiers. The Brenner Pass, located approximately 40 kilometers south of Innsbruck, has traditionally served as an important passage over the Alps, connecting Austria and Italy.

Historical Significance: The Brenner Pass has been an important crossing since Roman times, functioning as a vital commerce route connecting northern and southern Europe. Today, the pass serves as a key transportation route, but it is also a destination for exploring the region's rich history and culture. Visit the Europabrücke (Europe Bridge), one of Europe's tallest bridges, which crosses the pass and provides stunning views of the surrounding Alps.

Exploring the Italian Border: Once you cross the border into Italy, you'll be at the South Tyrol area, which is famed for its blend of Austrian and Italian culture. The first place you'll come across is Brenner, a little village that provides Italian-inspired shopping, eating, and cultural attractions. Enjoy a supper at a local trattoria, where you can sample Italian food with a Tirolean twist.

Sterzing/Vipiteno: The lovely village of Sterzing (Vipiteno in Italian) is only a short drive from the border. This medieval town is famous for its colorful architecture, ancient towers, and bustling marketplaces. Stroll around the town center, see the Zwölferturm (Twelve O'Clock Tower), and browse the shops and cafés that line the streets.

Scenic Drives and Views: The trip to the Brenner Pass is an adventure, with breathtaking vistas of the alpine scenery. Consider using the old Brenner road (B182) for a more scenic route that weaves through charming villages and provides several opportunities to stop and admire the views.

A day trip to the Brenner Pass and the Italian border is ideal for seeing the region's diverse cultures and scenery. Whether you're seeing historical monuments, sampling Italian food, or simply admiring the scenery, this tour provides a unique peek into the heart of the Alps.

These day tours from Innsbruck highlight the various sights and natural beauty that surround the city. Whether you enjoy art and culture, outdoor activity, or simply seeing new areas, these excursions are the ideal complement to your time in Innsbruck. Each place has its own distinct appeal, making it well worth the short trip from the city.

Innsbruck's Culinary Scene

Innsbruck is more than just a visual feast with its breathtaking mountain environment and ancient buildings; it's also a gastronomic paradise with a wide range of delicacies to enjoy. The city's cuisine culture is as diverse as its ethnic influences, combining traditional Tyrolean dishes with contemporary culinary trends. Whether you're a gourmet eager to sample local cuisine, a vegetarian searching for plant-based treats, or just someone who enjoys a nice cup of coffee, Innsbruck has something for everyone. In this chapter, we'll look at Innsbruck's gastronomic choices, including substantial Tyrolean dinners and the greatest cafés in town.

Traditional Tyrolean Dishes to Try

No visit to Innsbruck is complete without trying some of the region's typical cuisine. Tyrolean cuisine is noted for its substantial, warming dishes produced with locally sourced ingredients and tailored to sustain individuals who work and play in the mountains.

Käsespätzle: Käsespätzle, a traditional Tyrolean meal, is the Alpine version of macaroni and cheese. This delicious, creamy meal has spätzle (soft egg noodles) covered with melted cheese and crunchy onions. It's the ideal comfort dish after a day spent visiting the city or climbing in the mountains.

Tirolean Gröstl: This traditional farmer's dinner has grown popular among both residents and visitors. It's a one-pan meal made of fried potatoes, onions, and meat (typically beef or pig), which is frequently topped with a fried egg. It's easy, filling, and full of flavor.

Speckknödel: Another must-try delicacy is Speckknödel, a sort of bread dumpling filled with speck (smoked ham), onions, and herbs. These dumplings are typically served in a thick broth or with sauerkraut, resulting in a hearty dinner that embodies the region's rustic culinary traditions.

Kaiserschmarrn: Kaiserschmarrn, a fluffy, shredded pancake topped with powdered sugar and served with fruit compote or apple sauce, is a must-try dessert. This delicious dessert is named after Emperor Franz Joseph I of Austria and is popular in Tyrolean homes and restaurants.

These meals are only a handful of the typical cuisines available in Innsbruck, each providing a sense of the region's culinary heritage.

Best Restaurants in Innsbruck

Innsbruck's food scene is as diverse as it is good, with options ranging from modest mountain cabins to upscale restaurants. Here are some of the top places to eat in the city:

Die Wilderin: Situated in the heart of the Old Town, Die Wilderin is renowned for its farm-to-table philosophy, which employs exclusively locally produced foods. The menu varies often to reflect what is fresh and in season, but you can always count on inventive dishes that put a modern spin on traditional Tyrolean cuisine.

Lichtblick: For a dining experience with a view, visit Lichtblick, a rooftop restaurant that provides panoramic views of the city and Alps. The menu showcases contemporary Austrian cuisine, emphasizing local products and tastes. The contemporary, modern ambiance makes it ideal for a memorable evening out.

Gasthof Weisses Rössl: This ancient inn has been welcoming guests since the 15th century and is one of Innsbruck's most popular traditional eateries. You may enjoy traditional Tyrolean meals in a lovely, old-world environment. The warm wood-paneled dining rooms and pleasant service make it popular with both residents and visitors.

Schwarzer Adler: Another historic restaurant, Schwarzer Adler serves a combination of classic and contemporary food in an exquisite environment. The restaurant is part of a hotel that has been entertaining visitors since 1511, and the dining room's classy setting is suitable for a formal evening dinner.

These restaurants are simply the tip of the iceberg when it comes to discovering Innsbruck's gastronomic environment, which offers a delectable combination of history and innovation.

Street Food and Local Markets

Innsbruck's street food and local markets provide a more relaxed eating experience, showcasing the city's unique food culture.

Markthalle Innsbruck: The Markthalle is the city's major market hall, where you can find a variety of local products, meats, cheeses, and baked items. It's a terrific spot to pick up picnic items or try some fresh Tyrolean delicacies. Many of the kiosks also sell ready-to-eat foods, ranging from traditional sausages to artisan bread.

Food Truck Friday: If you're visiting Innsbruck on a Friday, don't miss Food Truck Friday, a weekly event where you can sample a variety of foreign and local street food. From gourmet burgers to Asian fusion, there's something for every taste. The event is popular among the locals and has a vibrant, sociable atmosphere.

Innsbruck Christmas Market: If you're visiting during the winter, don't miss the Innsbruck Christmas Market. While browsing the holiday kiosks, you may enjoy typical Tyrolean foods such as Kiachl (fried flatbread with sauerkraut or jam) and Glühwein (mulled wine). The market's pleasant atmosphere and delectable fragrances make it a Christmas season must-see.

These street food alternatives and markets provide a more casual approach to sample

Innsbruck's gastronomic wonders, ideal for a quick nibble or a leisurely eating excursion.

Vegetarian & Vegan Dining Options

Innsbruck is becoming more popular among vegetarians and vegans, with a rising number of eateries offering plant-based alternatives that do not sacrifice flavor.

Olive: A renowned vegetarian and vegan destination, Olive serves a diverse menu of plant-based cuisine produced with organic ingredients. The restaurant's friendly setting and emphasis on sustainability make it a popular choice among health-conscious guests.

My Indigo: This casual cafe serves vegetarian and vegan dishes influenced by world tastes. My Indigo serves a variety of bowls, salads, wraps, and curries, making it an ideal destination for a quick, nutritious dinner in the city center.

Vegan Bowls: As the name implies, Vegan Bowls specializes in plant-based bowl meals loaded with fresh veggies, grains, and protein. The menu is entirely vegan, and the meals are both nutritional and tasty, making it a popular choice for people looking for a healthy dinner.

These restaurants provide vegetarians and vegans lots of options when dining out in Innsbruck, with menus that highlight the diversity and originality of plant-based food.

Café Culture: The Best Coffee Houses

Innsbruck's café culture is an important aspect of the city's appeal, providing comfortable places to unwind with a coffee and croissant. Whether you choose a traditional Viennese café or a trendy coffee shop, Innsbruck has something for every coffee enthusiast.

Café Central: Café Central is a historic institution and one of Innsbruck's most well-known coffee establishments. With its exquisite décor and typical Viennese café ambiance, it's the ideal spot for a Melange (Austrian coffee) and a slice of Sachertorte. The café's prime position also makes it ideal for people-watching.

Kaffeehaus: Located near the University of Innsbruck, Kaffeehaus is a hot hangout for students and residents. The café provides high-quality coffee and a variety of handcrafted cakes and pastries. It's a terrific location to unwind because of its relaxed atmosphere and diverse décor.

Café Katzung: Located in the Old Town, Café Katzung provides a warm atmosphere with a menu that includes a range of coffee beverages, teas, and sweets. It's an excellent location for a mid-afternoon rest after visiting the neighboring sights.

These cafés are just a handful of the many excellent places in Innsbruck where you can relax with a cup of coffee while taking in the local ambiance.

Food Festivals & Culinary Events in 2024

Throughout the year, several food festivals and events bring Innsbruck's culinary scene to life, allowing visitors to sample local specialties and celebrate the city's gastronomic culture.

Innsbruck Food Festival: The Innsbruck Food Festival, held annually in the spring, exhibits the best of Tyrolean cuisine, with local chefs and producers exhibiting their greatest dishes. The event includes cooking demos, food vendors, and tastings, making it a must-see for culinary enthusiasts.

Kaiserweihnacht: This Christmas-themed culinary festival, held in December, highlights traditional Tyrolean holiday delicacies. Visitors may indulge in festive foods such as Lebkuchen (gingerbread), roasted chestnuts, and regional specialties while getting into the Christmas mood.

Alpenländische Festwochen: Held during the summer, this celebration celebrates Alpine culture via cuisine, music, and customs. The event has a variety of food vendors serving regional cuisine, as well as performances of traditional Tyrolean music and dance.

These events are an excellent way to discover Innsbruck's gastronomic diversity and immerse yourself in the city's thriving food culture.

Innsbruck's culinary culture reflects its rich cultural past and lively character. Whether you're indulging in traditional Tyrolean meals, discovering the city's bustling street food, or sipping a leisurely coffee at a historic café, Innsbruck has a delicious variety of flavors to offer. As you tour the city, let your taste sensations lead you to the best of Innsbruck.

Shopping in Innsbruck

Innsbruck, with its combination of classic elegance and modern flare, provides a shopping experience as varied as the city itself. From busy retail lanes lined with multinational brands to small specialized stores exhibiting local crafts, Innsbruck has something for every type of consumer. Whether you're looking for unusual souvenirs, browsing luxury stores, or simply taking in the ambiance at a local market, this chapter will walk you through the greatest shopping experiences Innsbruck has to offer.

Maria-Theresien-Straße

Maria-Theresien-Straße is Innsbruck's most popular shopping street, and it's simple to understand why. This lively street, named for Empress Maria Theresa, is the hub of the city's business center. It's an astonishing combination of old buildings and modern businesses, making it the ideal site to start your shopping trip.

International Brands: Along Maria-Theresien-Straße, you'll discover a wide range of international brands, from popular fashion outlets like Zara and H&M to luxury labels like Hugo Boss and Swarovski. This variety makes it simple to discover something for everyone, whether you're seeking current trends or classic items.

Historic Ambiance: One of the distinguishing features of shopping on Maria-Theresien-Straße is the contrast between modern retail outlets and the old building that surrounds them. As you peruse, take a minute to appreciate the Baroque facades and the majestic Arch of Triumph, which provide a regal touch to the shopping experience.

Cafés & Restaurants: After a few hours of shopping, you may relax at one of the numerous cafés and restaurants that line the street. Whether you want a quick coffee or a leisurely meal, there are plenty of alternatives. Many cafés have outside seating, enabling you to experience the colorful street bustle while relaxing.

Shopping on Maria-Theresien-Straße is more than simply a shopping experience; it allows you to immerse yourself in the vibrant ambiance of Innsbruck's city center.

Specialty Shops: Traditional Crafts and Souvenirs

For those looking for something genuinely unique, Innsbruck's specialized stores include a treasure trove of traditional crafts and souvenirs. These boutiques offer an insight into the region's rich cultural past and are ideal for finding unique presents.

Tyrolean Handicrafts: Innsbruck is famous for its Tyrolean crafts, which include finely carved wooden objects, traditional clothes, and elaborate lacework. *Handwerksladen*, for example, sells a diverse assortment of handcrafted items that make for authentic and meaningful keepsakes.

Swarovski Crystals: Wattens, home of the world-renowned Swarovski Crystal Worlds, is only a short drive from Innsbruck. However, you don't have to leave the city to find some stunning crystal items. The *Swarovski Innsbruck* store on Maria-Theresien-Straße is a must-see for anybody wishing to take home some glittering jewelry or decorative goods.

Traditional Attire: If you're looking for traditional Tyrolean clothes, or "Trachten," Innsbruck offers various establishments that specialize in these timeless pieces. Loden is a traditional option for people wishing to buy a dirndl, lederhosen, or a warm wool jacket. These things are not simply attractive, but also rooted in local customs.

Exploring Innsbruck's specialty stores is a fascinating opportunity to learn about the creativity and workmanship passed down through generations in Tyrol.

Shopping Malls & Boutiques

In addition to its picturesque streets and specialty businesses, Innsbruck has various shopping malls and boutiques that provide a more modern shopping experience. These stores provide a diverse range of things, including fashion and technology, all under one roof.

Sillpark Shopping Center: Sillpark, located in the city center, is one of Innsbruck's major retail malls. It has a combination of foreign and local brands, making it a handy destination to get everything you need in one location. Sillpark offers to all interests and budgets with a diverse range of shops, including apparel and accessories, home items, and technology.

DEZ Einkaufszentrum: A little further out from the city center, DEZ is another huge shopping mall with a varied assortment of retailers. DEZ is a popular attraction for residents, with a variety of stores, food options, and entertainment facilities. It's ideal for a full day of shopping.

Boutique Shopping: Innsbruck's boutique boutiques provide a more personal shopping experience. ***Boutique Petera*** provides high-end apparel in a trendy atmosphere, whilst ***Haller's*** is renowned for its carefully chosen range of local and worldwide brands. These tiny stores offer a more customized shopping experience and are great for locating one-of-a-kind items.

Innsbruck has lots to offer, whether you want to spend the day shopping or taking a leisurely stroll around boutique-lined alleys.

Farmers' Markets & Local Produce

Innsbruck's farmers' markets provide a more authentic and regionally oriented purchasing experience. These markets provide fresh, seasonal vegetables as well as a range of handcrafted crafts, giving visitors a taste of the area's agricultural riches.

Innsbruck Farmers' Market: Held weekly in the city center, the Innsbruck Farmers' Market is a thriving meeting of local farmers and producers. Here, you may get fresh fruits and vegetables, handcrafted cheeses, cured meats, and baked goodies. The market is an excellent spot to pick up picnic items or try some of the region's delicacies.

Markthalle Innsbruck: For a year-round market experience, go to the city's indoor

market hall. It is open every day and sells a variety of local and regional products, including fresh food and artisan handicrafts. The market hall also houses various food vendors where you may eat a meal produced with local products.

Seasonal Markets: Throughout the year, Innsbruck organizes a number of seasonal markets that showcase local goods and crafts. The Christmas Market is especially popular, with a beautiful array of seasonal snacks and homemade goods. The Easter Market, which takes place in the city center each spring, provides beautiful displays and seasonal cuisine.

Shopping at Innsbruck's farmers' markets is a great opportunity to explore the city's lively local culture while also supporting area suppliers.

Luxury Shopping & Designer Stores

Innsbruck has a variety of high-end businesses where you may shop for designer clothing, fine jewelry, and luxury items. These establishments provide a high-end shopping experience in attractive settings.

Swarovski Flagship Store: Beyond its renown for crystals, the Swarovski Flagship Store in Innsbruck provides a premium shopping experience with a large selection of jewelry, accessories, and home design goods. The store's sophisticated style and sumptuous displays make it a must-see for anybody interested in luxury products.

Rolex Boutique: For watch aficionados, the Rolex Boutique on Maria-Theresien-Straße is the place to visit. This store has a large collection of Rolex timepieces, each symbolizing the peak of Swiss workmanship. The store's skilled personnel provides exceptional service, assuring a high-end shopping experience.

Louis Vuitton: Louis Vuitton on Maria-Theresien-Straße specializes in premium handbags, luggage, and accessories. The store's clean, refined design, along with the renowned LV emblem, serve as a beacon for luxury consumers in Innsbruck.

Luxury shopping in Innsbruck blends the beauty of the city's historic backdrop with the best in modern design and workmanship to provide a genuinely sumptuous shopping experience.

Tips for Bargain Hunters

If you want to make the most of your shopping budget, Innsbruck offers several options for clever shoppers to get fantastic prices. Here are some ways to help you find the greatest deals:

Seasonal Sales: Like many European towns, Innsbruck has two main sale seasons each year: one in January and one in July. During these deals, you may get huge discounts on apparel, accessories, and other things, particularly at larger stores and malls.

Outlet Shopping: For even more discounts, consider visiting Designer Outlet Parndorf, which is located just outside of Innsbruck. This outlet mall provides savings on a wide range of international brands, including fashion and household items. It's worth the trip if you're looking for designer things at a discount.

Second-Hand and Vintage Shops: Innsbruck also offers a number of second-hand and vintage stores where you may get one-of-a-kind products at a lesser price. Carla Second-Hand and Vinzenzgemeinschaft are renowned bargain hunting destinations for apparel, accessories, and home décor products.

Tax-Free Shopping: If you are a non-EU resident, you can shop in Innsbruck without paying any taxes. Many shops provide VAT refunds for purchases exceeding a particular amount. Make sure you get a tax-free form at the time of sale and retain your receipts for a refund at the airport.

With these guidelines in mind, you may have a wonderful shopping trip in Innsbruck without breaking the wallet.

Innsbruck's shopping culture is as diverse as the city itself, with options for every taste and budget. Whether you're wandering down the lively Maria-Theresien-Straße, browsing specialist stores, or looking for discounts, you'll undoubtedly come across gems that represent the Alpine city's distinct character and charm.

Cultural Experiences & Events

Innsbruck is a city where culture and history merge with modern influences, creating a rich blend of experiences that draw people from all over the world. Throughout the year, the city holds a number of events to highlight its historical heritage, artistic accomplishments, and lively community spirit. Whether you enjoy music, theater, sports, or seasonal festivals, Innsbruck has cultural events that will make your vacation memorable. This chapter digs into some of the most memorable events and activities available during your time in Innsbruck.

The Innsbruck Festival of Early Music

The Innsbruck Early Music Festival is regarded as one of Europe's most significant festivals. This annual summer festival honors early music's rich legacy by bringing together world-renowned soloists and ensembles to play pieces from the Renaissance, Baroque, and early Classical periods.

Historical Venues: The event is held in some of Innsbruck's most attractive historic buildings, such as the Hofkirche (Court Church) and the Schloss Ambras. These settings not only provide magnificent acoustics, but they also take audiences back in time, increasing their musical experience.

Notable Performances: The festival's schedule often includes operas, concerts, and recitals that feature both well-known works and lesser-known early music gems. Previous editions featured Baroque operas by Handel and Vivaldi, as well as instrumental pieces by artists such as Monteverdi and Bach.

Workshops & Seminars: In addition to the concerts, the festival frequently hosts workshops, seminars, and masterclasses for musicians and researchers. These programs give a more in-depth understanding of the music and its historical context, making the festival a valuable experience for both artists and audiences.

The Innsbruck Festival of Early Music is a must-see for anybody interested in classical music and history, since it provides a one-of-a-kind opportunity to hear masterpieces played in their original settings.

Tiroler Volksschauspiele: Traditional Folk Performances

The Tiroler Volksschauspiele are a must-see for anybody looking to immerse themselves in true Tyrolean culture. This yearly event, held in the adjacent town of Telfs, honors the area's cultural traditions via theater, music, and dance.

Folk Theater: The Tiroler Volksschauspiele's main attraction is its folk theater performances. These performances, which are frequently based on local stories and historical events, are performed in the Tyrolean dialect and incorporate traditional costumes and music. The subjects span from humor to drama, with something for everyone's taste.

Local Participation: What distinguishes the Tiroler Volksschauspiele is the engagement of local communities. Many of the performers, singers, and dancers are locals who grew up with these customs, giving the shows a real and sincere feel.

Cultural Seminars: In addition to theater, the festival provides seminars and demonstrations in traditional Tyrolean crafts, music, and dance. These activities provide visitors a hands-on opportunity to interact with the region's cultural history.

Attending the Tiroler Volksschauspiele is a one-of-a-kind opportunity to engage with Tyrol's people and customs, as well as get insight into the region's rich cultural fabric.

Christmas Markets & Winter Festivals

Innsbruck is gorgeous in the winter, and its Christmas markets are a highlight of the holiday season. The city's lovely marketplaces, situated against the background of snow-capped mountains, are the ideal spot to get into the holiday mood.

Old Town Christmas Market: The most renowned of Innsbruck's Christmas markets takes place in the Old Town, beneath the magnificent Golden Roof. The market is recognized for its festive ambiance, with stalls offering handcrafted ornaments, traditional Tyrolean items, and seasonal delights such as mulled wine and roasted chestnuts.

Panorama Christmas Market: The Panorama Christmas Market in Hungerburg offers breathtaking views of the city. Accessible by funicular, this market provides a more private environment with fewer customers and a spectacular view of Innsbruck adorned by holiday lights.

Winter Festivals: Innsbruck's winter celebrations go beyond the Christmas market. The city offers a number of winter sports events, notably the renowned Four Hills Tournament at the Bergisel Ski Jump. There are also New Year's Eve events with fireworks and live music, as well as seasonal cultural shows.

Innsbruck's Christmas markets and winter festivities celebrate the season's warmth and enthusiasm, making it an excellent holiday destination.

The Bergisel Ski Jump: World Cup and Other Events

The Bergisel Ski Jump is not simply a symbol of Innsbruck, but also a world-class athletic site that stages important international events all year round. The ski jump, located on the city's outskirts, provides exhilarating competitions as well as stunning views of the surrounding mountains.

Four Hills Tournament: The most well-known event hosted at the Bergisel Ski Jump is the Four Hills Tournament, which is part of the FIS Ski Jumping World Cup. Every January, the world's top ski jumpers compete here, attracting big spectators and generating an electrifying environment. The event is a highlight of the winter sports calendar, with millions of viewers worldwide.

Year-Round Events: While the Four Hills Tournament is the major draw, the Bergisel Ski Jump conducts a variety of contests and events throughout the year. These include summer ski jumping competitions, where athletes prepare and compete on artificial surfaces, as well as cultural events such as concerts and exhibits.

Visitor Experience: Even if no competitions are taking place, the Bergisel Ski Jump is worth seeing. The complex features a museum about the history of ski jumping, as well as a panoramic café with breathtaking views of Innsbruck and the surrounding Alps.

The Bergisel Ski Jump is a must-see for sports aficionados, providing a unique perspective on the world of ski jumping, both past and present.

Summer Concerts & Open-Air Festivals

During the summer, Innsbruck comes alive with a variety of concerts and open-air festivals celebrating music, art, and community. These activities make use of the city's stunning outdoor venues and long summer evenings, resulting in a lively and friendly environment.

Innsbruck Promenade Concerts: The Innsbruck Promenade Concerts are held yearly in July and August in the courtyard of the Hofburg Imperial Palace. These free performances feature orchestras and musicians from all around the world playing a mix of classical, folk, and modern music. The environment, under the stars and surrounded by old architecture, provides a really unforgettable evening.

New Orleans Festival: Another highlight of the summer is the New Orleans Festival, which celebrates jazz and blues music in the heart of Innsbruck. The event features live performances by foreign and local performers, as well as food and beverage kiosks serving Southern-inspired cuisine.

Open-Air Cinema: For cinema enthusiasts, Innsbruck's Open-Air Cinema is a must-see. The festival, which takes place in a variety of places across the city, including the banks of the Inn River and the courtyard of the Landesmuseum, has a mix of classic and current films. The mix of movies and breathtaking outdoor locations produces an unforgettable cultural experience.

Innsbruck's summer activities provide a varied range of cultural experiences, making the city a popular summer vacation.

Year-Round Cultural Activities

Innsbruck's cultural environment is dynamic and diversified, with activities and events scheduled throughout the year. There is always something going on in this vibrant city, regardless of when you come.

Museums and Galleries: Innsbruck has various museums and galleries that provide year-round exhibitions and programming. The Tiroler Landesmuseum Ferdinandeum houses an extensive collection of art, history, and natural science displays, and the Kunstraum Innsbruck highlights contemporary art by local and international artists.

Theater and Dance: The Innsbruck State Theater (Tiroler Landestheater) hosts a diverse range of productions, including opera, ballet, drama, and concerts. The theater's schedule is jam-packed with shows ranging from ancient works to current ones, so there's always something to watch.

Traditional Events: Innsbruck's calendar also includes traditional events that highlight the region's cultural history. These include the Almabtrieb, an autumn celebration commemorating the return of livestock from alpine pastures, and Fasnacht, a spring Tyrolean carnival featuring colorful parades and masked dances.

Innsbruck's year-round cultural activities ensure that no matter when you visit, you can participate in the city's vibrant creative and cultural life.

Innsbruck's cultural offerings are both broad and numerous, making it a lively and energetic destination for tourists of all interests. From music festivals and traditional folk performances to world-class athletic events and seasonal celebrations, Innsbruck is a city that celebrates culture all year.

Family-Friendly Activities in Innsbruck

Innsbruck, set in the heart of the Alps, is not just a haven for outdoor enthusiasts and cultural fans; it is also an excellent choice for families. Innsbruck has a diverse range of activities for guests of all ages, including intriguing attractions, outdoor excursions, and family-friendly services. Whether you want to explore nature, learn something new, or simply have fun with your kids, this chapter will show you the greatest family-friendly activities in Innsbruck.

Visiting the Alpenzoo with Kids

The **Alpenzoo Innsbruck** is one of Europe's highest altitude zoos and an ideal family activity. This one-of-a-kind zoo, located on the slopes of the Nordkette Mountains, provides an intriguing look into Alpine fauna.

Alpine Animals: The zoo has about 2,000 animals representing 150 Alpine species. Your youngsters will be ecstatic to view lynxes, brown bears, wolves, ibex, and the elusive Alpine bearded vulture up close. The zoo's layout, which resembles natural ecosystems, provides an educational experience for youngsters, teaching them about the local ecology and conservation initiatives.

Interactive Exhibits: The Alpenzoo has various interactive displays meant to interest younger guests. The petting zoo, which allows youngsters to engage with friendly farm animals such as goats and lambs, is always popular. Additionally, the Fischotter Anlage (otter enclosure) allows children to see these lively creatures in action.

Stunning Views: The zoo's position provides spectacular views of Innsbruck, making it enjoyable for both children and parents. A trip to the Alpenzoo is easily linked with a ride on the *Hungerburgbahn* funicular, which provides an element of adventure for the entire family.

Visiting the Alpenzoo is more than simply a pleasant adventure; it also allows children to learn about the Alpine region's rich biodiversity in a setting that seems like a natural mountain hideaway.

Interactive Museums for Children

Innsbruck has various interactive museums geared at young brains, making learning a pleasant and hands-on experience.

Audioversum ScienceCenter: The Audioversum is a museum dedicated to the realm of sound and hearing. Its displays are extremely interactive, allowing youngsters to explore the science of sound in a fun and instructive way. The "Sound Lab" allows children to generate their own sounds, while other displays discuss the science of hearing and how our ears function. The museum frequently organizes special exhibitions geared at younger audiences, making it a good option for a wet day in Innsbruck.

Tyrolean Folk Art Museum: While not a children's museum, the Tyrolean Folk Art Museum has some entertaining exhibitions that will appeal to younger visitors. The museum's collection of traditional Tyrolean objects, including clothes, utensils, and furniture, is displayed in a way that brings history to life. Children may explore reconstructed historical settings and learn about life in Tyrol over the centuries. The museum also provides family tours and workshops where children may produce their own crafts inspired by Tyrolean customs.

Zeughaus Museum: The Zeughaus Museum (Armoury Museum) is another excellent choice for families, particularly those with youngsters who are interested in history. The museum's interactive exhibits on Tyrolean history from antiquity to the present day feature hands-on displays and multimedia presentations that make the past more accessible and entertaining for young visitors.

These museums provide excellent experiences that combine education and fun, keeping your children interested and curious during their stay.

Parks & Playgrounds in Innsbruck

Innsbruck is a city that loves its green areas, with several parks and playgrounds where families can rest and kids may play.

Rapoldi Park: Located in the city center, Rapoldipark is popular with families. The park has extensive green spaces, a duck pond, and various playgrounds with swings, slides, and climbing equipment. The park's layout promotes exploration, making it an ideal location for a family picnic or a leisurely stroll. The park's popularity grows during the summer, when it frequently holds outdoor events and festivals.

Hofgarten: The Hofgarten is a historic park next to the Imperial Palace that provides a peaceful environment for families to enjoy. The park has nicely planted gardens, a spacious playground, and a small pond where kids may observe fish and ducks. The playground is well-maintained and has equipment ideal for children of all ages. The Hofgarten's central position makes it an ideal stop for a day of touring.

Baggersee: Baggersee is a popular summer vacation location for families. This man made lake on the outskirts of Innsbruck has a beach, bathing areas, and lots of room for outdoor activities and picnics. The nearby park has a huge playground, as well as walking and bike routes. Baggersee is an ideal place to unwind and rest after a day of touring the city.

These parks and playgrounds offer plenty of opportunity for your children to burn off energy as you enjoy the beauty of Innsbruck's outdoor areas.

Family-Friendly Hiking Trails

The neighboring mountains of Innsbruck provide various family-friendly hiking paths suitable for all skill levels, guaranteeing that everyone can enjoy the breathtaking Alpine panorama.

The Zirbenweg Trail: A popular choice among families. This reasonably easy climb is located in the Patscherkofel region and provides panoramic views of the Inn Valley and the surrounding mountains. The track is well-marked and relatively level, making it ideal for kids and beginners. Along the path, information boards tell hikers about the local flora and animals, making it an educational experience as well.

The Muttereralm Family Adventure Trail: The Muttereralm is noted for its family-friendly ambiance and has an adventure path that children will enjoy. This route features interactive stations where kids can learn about the environment, construct miniature dams in streams, and climb on natural playgrounds. The Muttereralm also has a summer toboggan slide, which adds excitement to your hiking adventure.

The Arzler Alm Trail: This Trail is another excellent choice for families. This moderate climb leads to a classic Alpine lodge where you may eat and admire the scenery. The walk is ideal for small children, and the top destination includes a playground and petting zoo, offering lots of fun until you get to the Alm.

These routes provide an excellent balance of fitness, adventure, and stunning vistas, making them ideal for a family day out in the mountains.

Seasonal Activities for Kids

Regardless of the season, Innsbruck has a variety of activities suitable for children.

Winter Wonderland: In the winter, Innsbruck transforms into a snowy wonderland. Sledding, ice skating, and snowman construction are among the activities available in the city's parks for children. Several adjacent ski resorts provide ski schools particularly geared for children, so even the smallest family members may enjoy the excitement of skiing. Carousel rides and storytelling sessions are among the things available at Innsbruck's Christmas markets for youngsters.

Summer Fun: During the summer, Innsbruck's outdoor pools and lakes are popular destinations for families. Swimming, paddle boating, and picnics are popular activities on the Lanser and Natterer Sees. The city also offers a number of summer festivals featuring kid-friendly activities such as puppet shows, face painting, and interactive performances.

Spring & Autumn: Families may participate in seasonal events such as Easter egg hunts, harvest celebrations, and guided nature hikes. The botanical gardens and adjacent farms in Innsbruck provide educational excursions for children that are both enjoyable and informative.

These seasonal activities guarantee that there is always something fascinating for children to do, regardless of when they visit.

Tips for Traveling with Children

Traveling with children can be a wonderful experience, particularly in a family-friendly destination such as Innsbruck. Here are some ideas for a smooth and pleasurable trip:

Accommodation: Choose family-friendly lodgings that provide facilities like cribs, high chairs, and childcare. Many Innsbruck hotels provide family rooms or suites to ensure everyone's comfort.

Dining: Innsbruck's eateries are often family-friendly. Look for restaurants offering children's menus and outside seating, which may be more welcoming for young guests. Ask for tips on family-friendly restaurants.

Transportation: Innsbruck's public transit system is simple to use, especially with children. The buses and trams are stroller-friendly, and many sites are within walking distance of one another. Consider obtaining a family travel pass to ensure unrestricted access to public transportation throughout your stay.

Packing Essentials: Make sure to pack for the season, including proper clothes and outdoor equipment. Sunscreen, caps, and sunglasses are necessary in the summer, while warm layers and waterproof gear are required in the winter. Don't forget to carry snacks, drinks, and entertainment for the kids when traveling.

Plan Breaks: While it may be tempting to fill your agenda with activities, be sure to provide time for your children to relax. Allowing time for relaxation and play will keep them happy and involved during the trip.

With these suggestions, your family's trip to Innsbruck will be joyful, stress-free, and filled with great memories.

Innsbruck is a family-friendly city with a variety of activities for all ages. From the heights of the Alpenzoo to interactive museums and picturesque hiking routes, there are plenty of experiences for you and your children in this Alpine jewel.

Nightlife & Entertainment

Innsbruck is well-known for its magnificent scenery and outdoor experiences, but it also has a dynamic and diverse nightlife to suit everyone's preferences. Whether you're searching for a comfortable bar, an active nightclub, or a refined evening at the theater, Innsbruck's after-dark scene will not disappoint. This chapter delves into the finest of Innsbruck's nightlife, giving you a complete overview of the city's entertainment possibilities.

Bars and Pubs: Where to Enjoy a Drink

Innsbruck's bar culture is as diverse as its guests, ranging from classic Austrian pubs to fashionable cocktail bars. Whether you want a casual beer or a perfectly prepared drink, there is a place in Innsbruck to suit your needs.

Tribaun: Located in the heart of the city, Tribaun is popular with both locals and tourists. This intimate tavern serves an outstanding assortment of craft beers from across the world, with a special emphasis on local Austrian brews. The environment is relaxed, with rustic wooden decor and friendly personnel who are always eager to suggest a new brew to sample. Tribaun also organizes frequent live music evenings, giving it an ideal spot to unwind after a day of sightseeing.

Stiftskeller: For a more traditional experience, visit Stiftskeller, a historic beer hall in the Old Town. Stiftskeller, with its lofty ceilings, long oak tables, and hearty Austrian food, provides the ideal Innsbruck drinking experience. The pub offers a choice of local beers on tap as well as Austrian wines. It's the ideal place to unwind with friends over a pint of beer and schnitzel.

Liquid Diary: If you're looking for something a little more current, here is the place to be. This sleek cocktail bar, located near Maria-Theresien-Straße, is noted for its creative drink menu and contemporary decor. The bartenders here are genuine mixologists, creating one-of-a-kind drinks that are both visually appealing and tasty. Liquid Diary, with its elegant setting and large cocktail menu, is ideal for a classy night out.

These clubs and pubs provide a wide variety of experiences, ensuring that each night out in Innsbruck is unique.

Nightclubs & Live Music Venues

Innsbruck boasts a range of places that cater to diverse musical interests and atmospheres, so you may dance the night away or listen to live music.

Hofgarten Café: Located in Hofgarten Park, Hofgarten Café morphs from a pleasant daytime café to a raucous nightclub at night. The venue frequently presents DJ sets that include anything from electronic music to vintage hits. The dance floor is always full, and the outdoor terrace provides a more calm atmosphere for sipping a drink beneath the stars. Hofgarten Café is ideal for both residents and visitors wishing to enjoy Innsbruck's nightlife in a relaxed, energetic environment.

Weekender Club: The Weekender Club is a fixture on Innsbruck's live music scene. This legendary venue has hosted hundreds of musicians and DJs throughout the years, making it a must-see for music fans. The club's compact location and superb sound system make it ideal for watching live acts ranging from indie rock to electronic music. Weekender Club also offers themed evenings and special events, so there's always something interesting going on onstage.

PMK (Platform for Music and Culture): If you're into alternative music and underground scenes, this is the place to go. This location serves as a nexus for Innsbruck's artistic community, allowing both local and foreign artists to present their work. PMK's calendar is jam-packed with concerts, DJ sets, and cultural events spanning punk, metal, electronic, and experimental music. The venue's industrial appearance and edgy feel set it out as a nightlife destination.

Whether you prefer a relaxed live music experience or a wild night on the dance floor, Innsbruck's nightclubs and music venues provide something for everyone.

Theatre & Opera in Innsbruck

Innsbruck's cultural landscape comes alive in the evenings, with a variety of theatrical and opera acts that appeal to both specialists and casual fans. The city's venues host a variety of classic and modern shows, providing tourists with a varied cultural experience.

Tiroler Landestheater: The Tiroler Landestheater is Innsbruck's primary facility for theater, opera, and ballet. This ancient theater, near the Hofburg, is well-known for its high-quality plays and exquisite architecture. The theater's programming ranges from classic operas such as Verdi's La Traviata to current plays and dance shows. Attending a concert at the Tiroler Landestheater is a terrific chance to experience local culture while also having a refined night out.

Kammerspiele: The Kammerspiele provides a more intimate theatrical experience by hosting a range of acts in a smaller, more personal environment. This theater is noted for its avant-garde shows and unique stage design, which frequently include works by current authors and experimental theater companies. The Kammerspiele's inventive approach to theater makes it a popular choice for visitors searching for something unique.

Haus der Musik: The Haus der Musik is Innsbruck's primary venue for musical events, including opera, classical concerts, and chamber music. The facility holds concerts by the Tyrolean Symphony Orchestra and other prominent ensembles, making it a must-see for music enthusiasts. The Haus der Musik also provides pre-performance discussions and seminars, which deepen your understanding of the music and enhance your entire experience.

These venues provide a variety of alternatives for anyone wishing to enjoy a night of high culture in Innsbruck, with performances to suit both conventional and modern tastes.

Evening Walks & Scenic Spots

For those who prefer a more relaxing evening, Innsbruck has various beautiful places and lovely walks that are ideal for taking in the city's charm after dark.

Innsbruck Old Town: Taking an evening stroll around Innsbruck's Old Town is like going back in time. The medieval alleyways are wonderfully lighted, and many ancient monuments, like the Golden Roof and Hofburg Palace, are bathed in gentle lighting, creating a lovely scene. The quieter nighttime hours allow you to fully appreciate the architecture's fine features as well as the beauty of the small alleyways.

Innbrücke and the River Inn: For a calm walk with spectacular views, visit the Innbrücke bridge, which spans the River Inn. The bridge provides panoramic views of the city and neighboring mountains, especially when the sun sets behind the Alps. A walk down the riverside is another great opportunity to enjoy Innsbruck's natural beauty, with the soft murmur of the river providing a peaceful background.

Hungerburg and the Nordkette: For an unforgettable nighttime experience, ride the Hungerburgbahn funicular up to the Hungerburg and Nordkette mountains. From here, you can see panoramic views of Innsbruck as the city lights glimmer below. There are various picturesque areas where you can sit and enjoy the view, or if you want to be more daring, head up to Seegrube for a starlit trek or a drink at the summit café.

These nighttime walks are a peaceful and romantic way to explore Innsbruck, giving an excellent contrast to the city's more active nightlife alternatives.

Casino Innsbruck

For those wishing to liven up their evening, Casino Innsbruck provides a sophisticated and stylish backdrop for a night out. This casino, located in the city center, is one of Austria's most well-known gambling attractions.

Gaming Experience: Casino Innsbruck has a diverse selection of gambling alternatives, including roulette, blackjack, poker, and a number of slot machines. Whether you're a seasoned gambler or just seeking to try your luck, the casino's beautiful and relaxing ambiance provides an entertaining experience. The staff is kind and eager to explain the rules to newbies, ensuring that everyone may participate in the fun.

Dining and Entertainment: In addition to its gaming options, Casino Innsbruck has a fantastic restaurant and bar where you can have a gourmet meal or a beverage before heading to the gaming floor. The casino also offers special events, such as live music performances, themed evenings, and poker tournaments, to provide entertainment outside of the gaming tables.

Dress Code and Etiquette: Although Casino Innsbruck has a more liberal dress code than most European casinos, it is nevertheless recommended to dress appropriately. For males, a blazer is advised, while ladies should dress smart casual. The casino's pleasant and competent personnel make your evening pleasurable and comfortable.

Whether you're seeking for a night of gaming or just want to soak up the casino's dynamic ambiance, Casino Innsbruck provides a fashionable and thrilling alternative for your evening in the city.

Innsbruck's nightlife and entertainment culture is as broad and vibrant as the city itself. From comfortable pubs and bustling nightclubs to exquisite theaters and gorgeous nighttime walks, there is something for everyone to enjoy once the sun goes down. Whether you want a calm drink, a cultural show, or an exciting night out, Innsbruck has limitless options for a fantastic evening.

Wellness and Relaxation

Innsbruck, located in the gorgeous Austrian Alps, is more than simply an adventure and culture hotspot; it's also a paradise for people looking for wellness and leisure. Whether you want to unwind in a magnificent spa, immerse in the therapeutic waters of a thermal bath, or discover inner peace via yoga and meditation, Innsbruck has a range of activities to suit your needs. This chapter will walk you through the greatest possibilities for leisure and self-care in Innsbruck, making your holiday as rejuvenating as it is fun.

Spas and Wellness Centers

Innsbruck has a plethora of top-tier spas and wellness facilities that promise to relax both body and mind. These facilities combine ancient Alpine health techniques with contemporary therapies to provide an unmatched experience of relaxation and regeneration.

aDLERS Hotel Spa: Situated in the center of Innsbruck, the aDLERS Hotel Spa provides a magnificent hideaway with breathtaking panoramic views of the surrounding Alps. The spa offers a variety of services, including massages, facials, and body wraps, all meant to relieve tension and restore your body. The spa's feature is its rooftop sauna and relaxation area, which offers stunning views of the Alps. After your treatment, grab a drink at the spa's bar or unwind in the indoor pool.

Aqua Dome Spa: Located only a short drive from Innsbruck, the Aqua Dome Spa in Längenfeld is a world-class wellness center not to be missed. Aqua Dome is known for its modern architecture and vast range of services, which provide a full health experience. The spa's thermal pools, which are filled with warm, mineral-rich water, are perfect for soothing fatigued muscles. The spa also has saunas, steam tubs, and a separate wellness section with treatments based on the therapeutic powers of the Alps. Aqua Dome is ideal for a day excursion, enabling you to relax in a peaceful atmosphere surrounded by nature.

Lanserhof Lans: For a more tailored wellness experience, Lanserhof Lans provides medical spa treatments that mix traditional healing methods with cutting-edge therapies. Located in a beautiful location just outside of Innsbruck, this wellness facility is well-known for its holistic approach to health, which includes detox programs, stress management, and preventative treatment. The spa's treatments are tailored to each guest's specific requirements, delivering a genuinely soothing experience. Lanserhof Lans is suitable for individuals who want to unwind while also improving their general health.

These spas and wellness facilities offer the ideal retreat from the stresses of daily life, enabling you to indulge in some much-needed self-care.

Thermal Baths and Hot Springs

Thermal baths and hot springs have been valued for generations for their medicinal effects, and Innsbruck and its surroundings provide several opportunities to enjoy these natural wonders.

Therme Völs: Located near Innsbruck, Therme Völs is a popular location for individuals looking for thermal water's medicinal effects. Natural hot springs provide the baths with minerals that are claimed to promote relaxation and healing. The facility has many pools, each at a different temperature, allowing you to select the ideal setting for your requirements. Therme Völs also has a sauna and a variety of wellness treatments, making it an excellent choice for a day of leisure.

Bad Häring Thermal Spa: Located in the lovely Tyrolean countryside, the Bad Häring Thermal Spa is another fantastic choice for people wishing to enjoy the advantages of thermal waters. The resort is famous for its warm, sulfur-rich waters, which are thought to have healing effects, particularly for joint and muscular problems. In addition to the thermal pools, the spa provides a number of therapeutic therapies, such as mud baths and hydrotherapy. Bad Häring's calm surroundings and serene ambiance make it an ideal place for relaxation.

Alpentherme Gastein: Despite being a little further from Innsbruck, Alpentherme Gastein is worth the drive for its extensive wellness options. The thermal spa is located in the Gastein Valley, which is famous for its unique radon-rich waters, which are considered to offer several health advantages. The facility includes indoor and outdoor hot pools, saunas, and a rest area with breathtaking mountain views. Alpentherme also provides a variety of therapies, including radon therapy, which is said to enhance circulation and reduce chronic pain.

These thermal baths and hot springs provide a natural and refreshing approach to complement your health vacation in Innsbruck.

Yoga and Meditation Retreats

Innsbruck's calm atmosphere makes it a great site for yoga and meditation retreats, allowing you to reconnect with yourself and find inner peace amidst the splendor of the Alps.

Yoga Shala Innsbruck: Yoga Shala Innsbruck provides a tranquil refuge in the city center, as well as a range of yoga courses for all skill levels. The studio's expert teachers will walk you through exercises to increase your flexibility, strength, and mental clarity. Whether you're an experienced yogi or a novice, Yoga Shala Innsbruck provides a warm atmosphere in which to enhance your practice. The studio also offers workshops and meditation classes, which allow you to learn about many elements of yoga and mindfulness.

Mountain Yoga Retreats: For a more immersive experience, try attending a mountain yoga retreat in the nearby Alps. These retreats incorporate yoga practice, hiking, meditation, and other outdoor activities to provide a comprehensive approach to healing. The retreats are frequently conducted in tranquil settings with breathtaking mountain views, allowing you to reconnect with nature while nourishing your body and mind. The mix of physical exercise, mindful meditation, and natural beauty makes these retreats genuinely transforming.

Silent Meditation Retreats: If you want to enhance your meditation practice, Innsbruck offers silent retreats where you may completely detach from the outside world and focus on your inner journey. These retreats are frequently held at secluded monasteries or mountain lodges, which provide a peaceful environment for reflection. Guided meditation sessions, mindfulness exercises, and moments of solitude can help you achieve inner calm and clarity. Whether you're new to meditation or want to improve your practice, a silent retreat may be a deeply enlightening experience.

Yoga and meditation retreats in Innsbruck provide an excellent opportunity to restore your mind, body, and soul, leaving you feeling rejuvenated and focused.

Health and Fitness Facilities

For people who enjoy being active while on vacation, Innsbruck has a variety of health and fitness facilities to suit all fitness levels.

Vitalis Fitness Center: Located in the city center, Vitalis Fitness Center is a cutting-edge facility with a diverse selection of workout equipment and programs. Whether you like strength training, aerobic exercises, or group fitness courses like spinning and Pilates, Vitalis provides everything you need to keep active during your visit. The facility also has a wellness section with a sauna and steam room, where you may relax and recover after a workout.

Innsbruck Climbing Center: For those seeking a more adventurous workout, the Innsbruck Climbing Center provides an indoor climbing facility that welcomes climbers of all ability levels. The facility has a variety of climbing walls, including bouldering sections and top-rope routes, which offer a hard and enjoyable way to keep active. The facility also provides introductory climbing training, making it accessible to all levels of experience.

Olympiaworld Innsbruck: Olympiaworld Innsbruck is a multi-sport facility that provides a wide range of training and leisure opportunities. The complex has an ice rink, a swimming pool, a gym, tennis courts, and a track and field area. Olympiaworld offers a variety of activities, including swimming, skating, and weightlifting. The facility also provides fitness courses and personal trainer services, allowing you to keep your fitness regimen while on vacation.

These health and fitness facilities allow you to keep active and healthy while seeing everything Innsbruck has to offer.

Relaxation Spots in Nature

Innsbruck's natural beauty offers several options for leisure in the great outdoors. Whether you prefer a calm walk in the park or a quiet time by a mountain lake, there are lots of places to relax and enjoy nature's peacefulness.

Hofgarten: The Hofgarten, located in the city center, is a historic park that provides a calm respite from the urban buzz. Hofgarten's well groomed gardens, shady walks, and serene ponds make it ideal for a leisurely stroll or a quiet period of introspection. The park also has various seats and picnic spots, making it an excellent spot for a quiet afternoon.

Lake Natterer See: Just a short drive from Innsbruck, Lake Natterer See is a beautiful place to rest and unwind. The lake is bordered by thick forests and rolling hills, creating a tranquil environment for swimming, sunbathing, or simply admiring the scenery. There are also various walking routes surrounding the lake that allow you to discover the area's natural beauty at your own speed.

Patscherkofel Mountain: For a more immersive nature experience, visit Patscherkofel Mountain, which has various gorgeous sites ideal for relaxing. Whether you're taking a break on a hike or having a picnic with a view, the tranquil surroundings and pure mountain air will revive your spirit. The mountain's cable car makes it simple to reach these locations, allowing you to appreciate the majesty of the Alps without the exertion of a complete trek.

These natural relaxation areas in and around Innsbruck provide a calm hideaway where you may unwind and recharge while surrounded by the grandeur of the Austrian Alps.

Innsbruck is more than simply a place for adventure and culture; it is also a haven for people seeking wellness and leisure. From exquisite spas and curative thermal baths to calm yoga retreats and peaceful natural surroundings, Innsbruck provides a wide range of experiences that cater to your well-being, leaving you feeling refreshed and renewed.

Practical Information for Travelers

When planning a vacation to Innsbruck, it's critical to provide yourself with practical information that will make your stay easier, more enjoyable, and stress-free. This chapter includes everything from financial advice and linguistic instructions to emergency numbers and connection alternatives. Whether you're traveling single or with friends and family, this section will help you traverse Innsbruck with ease.

Currency, Banking and ATMs

Currency: Austria is a member of the Eurozone, hence the official currency in Innsbruck is the Euro (€). The euro is split into 100 cents. The most regularly used denominations are €5, €10, €20, and €50 notes, with €1 and €2 coins being used for minor transactions.

Banking: Innsbruck has a strong financial system, with branches of major banks like Erste Bank, Raiffeisen, and UniCredit conveniently located across the city. Most banks are open Monday through Friday, normally from 8:00 a.m. to 3:00 p.m., however some may shut early on Fridays or have longer hours on specific days.

ATMs: ATMs (known locally as "Bankomats") are extensively available in Innsbruck, particularly in the city center, commercial districts, and near important attractions. Most ATMs accept foreign debit and credit cards, including Visa, MasterCard, and Maestro. When withdrawing cash, you may be given the option of converting the amount to your native currency; it is normally best to refuse this option and complete the transaction in euros to avoid unfavorable exchange rates.

Currency Exchange: While ATMs are the most convenient way to obtain euros, you may also exchange money at currency exchange offices, banks, and some hotels. However, conversion rates at airports and hotels may be less beneficial than those at banks and dedicated currency exchange offices in the city core.

Language Tips & Common Phrases

Language: German is the official language of Innsbruck and across Austria. While many residents speak English, particularly in tourist regions, learning a few basic German words can help you have a more authentic experience and connect with the culture. Here are a few useful phrases.

- Hello/Goodbye: Hallo/Auf Wiedersehen
- Please / Thank you: Bitte/Danke
- Yes/No: Ja/Nein
- Excuse me / Sorry: Entschuldigung / Es tut mir leid
- Do you speak English?: Sprechen Sie Englisch?
- How much does this cost?: Wie viel kostet das?
- Where is...?: Wo ist...?
- I would like...: Ich hätte gerne...
- The bill, please: Die Rechnung, bitte
- Help!: Hilfe!

Pronunciation Tips: Austrian German has subtleties and may differ significantly from standard German. However, people applaud any attempt to speak their language, no matter how rudimentary. Remember to pronounce words accurately and listen to the local intonation, which may help you learn more about the language throughout your stay.

Language Apps: If you're concerned about the language barrier, consider installing a translation or language learning app such as Duolingo or Babbel. These may be quite useful for rapid translations and learning phrases on the move.

Emergency Contacts and Health Services

Emergency Numbers: Although Innsbruck is a safe city, it is always a good idea to be prepared. The following emergency numbers are critical to your safety:

- General Emergency (Police, Fire, Ambulance): 112 (this is the European-wide emergency number)
- Police: 133
- Fire Department: 122
- Ambulance/Medical Emergency: 144
- Mountain Rescue (Alpine Emergencies): 140

Health Services: Innsbruck has a comprehensive healthcare system, with various hospitals and clinics. For non-emergency medical difficulties, you can see a general practitioner (GP) or an outpatient clinic (Ambulanz). Most physicians speak English, but it's best to ask for one when scheduling an appointment.

- University Hospital Innsbruck (Universitätskliniken Innsbruck): The city's primary hospital, it provides comprehensive medical care and is well-equipped to manage emergencies.
- Pharmacies (Apotheken): Pharmacies are widely available in Innsbruck and are well-stocked with prescription and over-the-counter drugs. Look for the green cross, which signals a pharmacy. A few pharmacies provide after-hours service on a rotating basis, and you may discover the nearest one by checking the list posted in any drugstore.

Travel Insurance: It is strongly advised that you get travel insurance that covers health, accidents, and theft when visiting Austria. In the event of a medical emergency, having insurance ensures that you obtain the essential care without concern about the expense.

Internet and Mobile Connectivity

Wi-Fi: Innsbruck is a well-connected city with free Wi-Fi in many public places, including the city center, tourist information offices, cafés, and hotels. Look for signage advertising free Wi-Fi zones, or ask the venue for the password. Many cafés and restaurants also provide free

Wi-Fi to customers, making it simple to stay connected during your visit.

Mobile Connectivity: Austria has great mobile network coverage, including Innsbruck. If you want to use your phone regularly for calls, data, or navigation, you should consider getting a local SIM card. A1, T-Mobile, and Drei are three of Austria's major mobile providers. SIM cards are accessible at mobile phone stores, supermarkets, and even some vending machines at the airport. Before you purchase a local SIM, make sure your phone is unlocked.

Data Roaming: Thanks to EU roaming restrictions, you may use your phone as if you were at home. If you're going from outside the EU, ask your carrier about roaming fees or consider utilizing a local SIM card or a mobile Wi-Fi hotspot.

Internet Cafes: Although not as prevalent as they once were, there are still a few internet cafes in Innsbruck, notably around the university. These are useful if you need to access the internet without your own device.

Innsbruck for Solo Travelers: Safety and Tips

Safety: Innsbruck is a highly safe city for single travelers. The crime rate is low, and the city is well-policed, making it a safe area to explore on your own. However, it's always advisable to take common-sense precautions:

- ***Stay in well-lit places at night:*** Innsbruck is secure, but like any other city, it's better to stay in well-lit, crowded areas after midnight.
- ***Be mindful of your belongings:*** Pickpocketing is uncommon, although it can occur in busy settings such as markets or festivals. Keep your things safe, and be cautious of your surroundings.
- ***Use reputable transportation:*** If you take a cab, be sure it comes from a licensed business. Solo travelers will find Innsbruck's public transportation to be dependable and safe.

Meeting People: Solo travel does not need you to be alone. Innsbruck has several options to meet other visitors and locals:

- ***Hostels & social accommodations:*** Staying at a hostel or guesthouse is an excellent opportunity to meet other

tourists. Many of these places provide group activities and trips.
- ***Join group tours:*** Innsbruck provides several guided tours that are ideal for single visitors. Whether it's a walking tour of the Old Town or a hike in the mountains, these programs provide a social setting while also enabling you to explore.
- ***Attend events & workshops:*** Look into local events, workshops, and language exchange groups. These are great opportunities to meet new people and learn about Innsbruck's culture.

Self-Care: Solo travel may be extremely gratifying, but it's important to take care of yourself.

- ***Pace yourself:*** With so much to see and do, it's easy to get burnt out. Set aside time for rest and relaxation, whether it's a quiet day at a café or a day at the spa.
- ***Stay connected:*** Inform someone about your vacation intentions, especially if you're going on a trek or visiting distant locations. Keep your phone charged, and consider bringing a portable charger.

- ***Embrace solitude:*** One of the benefits of solo travel is the ability to explore at your own speed. Take use of this to enjoy moments of isolation, such as trekking in the Alps or reflecting in a peaceful park.

Innsbruck is a pleasant and welcoming location for all guests, even those traveling alone. By familiarizing yourself with the practical facts in this chapter, you will be able to explore the city with ease, assuring a safe, pleasurable, and memorable stay in this magnificent Alpine treasure.

Sample Itineraries

Innsbruck is a destination that caters to all types of travelers, from those seeking a quick weekend escape to families looking for a week-long adventure. Planning your trip can be overwhelming with so much to see and do, so we've crafted a few sample itineraries to help you make the most of your time in this stunning Alpine city. Whether you're here for a short stay or an extended vacation, these itineraries offer a perfect blend of sightseeing, culture, outdoor activities, and relaxation.

Weekend Getaway Itinerary

Day 1: Arrival & Old Town Exploration

- *Morning:* Arrive in Innsbruck and settle into your accommodation. If you're staying near the city center, start your exploration with a leisurely stroll through Innsbruck's Old Town. Begin at Maria-Theresien-Straße, the city's bustling main street, where you can admire the historic buildings and soak up the vibrant atmosphere.
- *Late Morning:* Visit the iconic Golden Roof (Goldenes Dachl), Innsbruck's most famous landmark, and explore the

museum inside to learn about the city's history. Nearby, the Innsbruck City Tower (Stadtturm) offers panoramic views of the Old Town and the surrounding mountains.
- **Lunch:** Enjoy a traditional Tyrolean lunch at one of the cozy restaurants in the Old Town. Don't miss trying Gröstl (a hearty potato dish) or Käsespätzle (cheese noodles).
- **Afternoon:** Head to the Hofburg Imperial Palace for a guided tour. This historic palace offers a glimpse into the life of the Habsburg rulers, with opulent rooms and impressive collections of art and artifacts.
- **Evening:** End your day with a leisurely walk along the Inn River, followed by dinner at a riverside restaurant. If you're in the mood for nightlife, visit one of the local bars or pubs for a drink.

Day 2: Nature and Culture

- **Morning:** Take the Nordkette cable car from the city center up to the Nordkette Mountains. Spend the morning hiking or simply enjoying the breathtaking views of Innsbruck and the surrounding

Alps from the top. If you're visiting in winter, skiing is a must.
- **Lunch:** Have lunch at one of the mountain huts, where you can savor Tyrolean specialties with a view.
- **Afternoon:** Return to the city and visit the Tiroler Landesmuseum Ferdinandeum. This museum houses an extensive collection of Tyrolean art and cultural artifacts, offering a deeper understanding of the region's heritage.
- **Evening:** Enjoy a cultural evening by attending a classical concert or a performance at the Tiroler Landestheater. Alternatively, explore Innsbruck's vibrant restaurant scene, with options ranging from traditional Austrian cuisine to international flavors.

One-Week Adventure Itinerary

Day 1: Arrival & Old Town Highlights

- **Morning:** Arrive in Innsbruck and take some time to relax at your hotel. Begin your adventure with a visit to the Golden Roof and the City Tower to get an overview of the city.
- **Afternoon:** Explore the Hofburg Imperial Palace and then take a leisurely

stroll along Maria-Theresien-Straße, stopping at cafes and boutiques.
- *Evening:* Dine at a traditional Austrian restaurant and take a scenic evening walk along the Inn River.

Day 2: Nature and Outdoor Activities

- *Morning:* Take the Nordkette cable car for a day of outdoor activities. Depending on the season, go hiking, skiing, or snowboarding in the Nordkette Mountains.
- *Afternoon:* Continue exploring the mountains or return to Innsbruck for a relaxing afternoon at the Alpenzoo, where you can see animals native to the Alpine region.
- *Evening:* Unwind with dinner at a local tavern, enjoying hearty Tyrolean dishes.

Day 3: Day Trip to Swarovski Crystal Worlds

- *Morning:* Take a day trip to the nearby town of Wattens to visit the Swarovski Crystal Worlds. This unique museum and art installation is a must-see for anyone interested in art, design, and craftsmanship.

- *Afternoon:* After exploring the museum, return to Innsbruck and visit the Imperial Palace Museum for more cultural insights.
- *Evening:* Spend the evening at one of Innsbruck's cozy wine bars or cafés.

Day 4: Exploring the Surrounding Villages

- *Morning:* Take a trip to Seefeld in Tirol, a charming village known for its beautiful landscapes and outdoor activities. Spend the morning hiking or exploring the village.
- *Afternoon:* Visit the medieval town of Hall in Tirol, where you can wander through its well-preserved streets and visit the Mint Tower.
- *Evening:* Return to Innsbruck and enjoy dinner at a restaurant specializing in Tyrolean cuisine.

Day 5: Innsbruck's Museums & Galleries

- *Morning:* Spend the day exploring Innsbruck's museums, starting with the Tiroler Landesmuseum Ferdinandeum. Afterward, visit the Grassmayr Bell

Museum to learn about the art of bell making.
- *Afternoon:* Explore local art at one of Innsbruck's contemporary galleries, such as the Taxispalais Kunsthalle Tirol.
- *Evening:* Attend a performance at the Tiroler Landestheater or enjoy a relaxing evening at one of Innsbruck's many cafés.

Day 6: Adventure Sports and Relaxation

- *Morning:* Experience the thrill of paragliding over Innsbruck or try your hand at mountain biking on one of the many scenic trails.
- *Afternoon:* After an adrenaline-filled morning, unwind at a local spa or wellness center. You can also visit the thermal baths in nearby villages for a soothing experience.
- *Evening:* Dine at a high-end restaurant in Innsbruck, enjoying a meal that blends traditional and modern Austrian cuisine.

Day 7: Final Day and Departure

- *Morning:* Spend your last day visiting any attractions you may have missed or

taking a final stroll through the Old Town. Consider visiting the Innsbruck Cathedral for a moment of reflection before you depart.
- *Afternoon:* Enjoy a leisurely lunch and do some last-minute shopping for souvenirs on Maria-Theresien-Straße.
- *Evening:* Depending on your departure time, spend the evening at a café or take in one last view of the city from the top of the City Tower before heading to the airport or train station.

Family Vacation Itinerary

Day 1: Arrival and Relaxation

- *Afternoon:* Arrive in Innsbruck and settle into a family-friendly hotel. Take it easy on your first day with a relaxing stroll through the Old Town, where kids can marvel at the Golden Roof and the lively street performers.
- *Evening:* Enjoy a family dinner at a restaurant that caters to children, offering both traditional Tyrolean dishes and kid-friendly options.

Day 2: Alpine Zoo and Interactive Museums

- *Morning:* Start your day with a visit to the Alpenzoo, one of Europe's highest zoos. The kids will love seeing animals native to the Alps, including ibexes, lynxes, and brown bears.
- *Afternoon:* After lunch, head to the Audioversum ScienceCenter, an interactive museum where children can engage with science and technology through hands-on exhibits.
- *Evening:* Treat the family to a casual dinner at a pizzeria or a local restaurant with a play area.

Day 3: Family-Friendly Hiking and Outdoor Fun

- *Morning:* Take the Nordkette cable car up to the mountains for a family-friendly hike. The trails around the Seegrube station are ideal for children and offer stunning views.
- *Afternoon:* Enjoy a picnic with a view, then let the kids burn off some energy at the mountain playgrounds.

- ***Evening:*** Return to Innsbruck and enjoy a quiet evening at your hotel or take a family walk along the Inn River.

Day 4: Day Trip to the Stubai Glacier

- ***Morning:*** Embark on a day trip to the Stubai Glacier, where the whole family can enjoy year-round snow fun. From skiing and snowboarding to snowshoeing and ice cave explorations, there's something for everyone.
- ***Afternoon:*** Have lunch at one of the glacier's panoramic restaurants, offering breathtaking views of the surrounding mountains.
- ***Evening:*** Return to Innsbruck and enjoy a family movie night at your hotel or a local cinema.

Day 5: Exploring Innsbruck's Parks and Playgrounds

- ***Morning:*** Spend the day exploring Innsbruck's parks, such as Rapoldi Park or the Botanical Garden. These green spaces are perfect for a relaxing day outdoors, with plenty of playgrounds for the kids to enjoy.

- ***Afternoon:*** Visit the nearby Ambras Castle, where children can explore the grounds and learn about medieval history.
- ***Evening:*** End the day with a family-friendly dinner at a restaurant that offers a special children's menu.

Day 6: Interactive Fun and Farewell

- ***Morning:*** Visit another family-friendly museum, such as the Tirol Panorama Museum, where kids can engage with exhibits on Tyrolean history and culture.
- ***Afternoon:*** Let the kids have some fun at a local indoor playground or visit the Hofgarten, a beautiful garden with plenty of space to run around.
- ***Evening:*** For your final night, have a special family dinner at a restaurant with traditional Austrian cuisine and a welcoming atmosphere for children.

Day 7: Departure

- ***Morning:*** Depending on your departure time, spend the morning visiting any last-minute sights or doing some final shopping for souvenirs.

- ***Afternoon:*** Pack up and say goodbye to Innsbruck, with memories of a fantastic family vacation that everyone will cherish.

These itineraries are designed to help you experience the best of Innsbruck, whether you're visiting for a short weekend or a longer stay. With its mix of history, culture, and outdoor activities, Innsbruck offers something for every traveler, ensuring that your visit is as enjoyable and memorable as possible.

Conclusion

Innsbruck, with its rich history, dynamic culture, and breathtaking natural surroundings, creates an indelible impact on every visitor. Innsbruck has something very special to offer, whether you're drawn to the gorgeous Alps, captivated by the city's imperial heritage, or anxious to experience the Tyrolean people's warm welcome.

As you progress through this tour, it becomes evident that Innsbruck is much more than just a scenic stopover in the center of the Alps. It's a city where modernity and tradition coexist, where outdoor activities are as easily accessible as world-class cultural events, and where every turn reveals something new and intriguing. From the lively streets of the Old Town to the peaceful paths of the surrounding Alps, Innsbruck welcomes exploration and discovery.

This guide is intended to assist you in navigating the numerous sides of Innsbruck, ensuring that you get the most out of your visit. Whether you followed one of the suggested itineraries or carved your own path, we hope you found this information useful in making your vacation to Innsbruck really unforgettable.

However, the charm of Innsbruck does not cease with your visit. The memories of your stay here—the breathtaking vistas, the tasty Tyrolean meals, and the warm atmosphere—will linger with you long after you leave. Innsbruck has a way of drawing tourists back, delivering something new with each visit, whether it's a new season or an undiscovered area of the city.

As you close your voyage in Innsbruck, carry with you the spirit of exploration and admiration for the diverse cultures, history, and landscapes that make this city special. Whether you leave with intentions to return or with a sense of accomplishment from seeing what you set out to see, know that Innsbruck has enhanced your travel experiences.

Thank you for including this guide as part of your Innsbruck journey. May your recollections of this wonderful city motivate you to go farther and connect more deeply with the world around you. Safe travels, and we will meet again in the heart of the Alps!

Printed in Great Britain
by Amazon

59428773R00086